SNO-CONE DIARIES

Sno-Cone Diaries

A sweet route to happiness

Watercolor by Matt Legge

SNO-CONE DIARIES
A Sweet Route to Happiness

ABBY VEGA

First Edition
ISBN: 978-0-9814795-9-0
Cover image by Kate Gundersen
Author photo by Danielle Brehm Photography
Watercolor (front matter) and "Breaking Point" illustration (p. 12) by Matthew Legge
Printed in the United States of America
Editorial, design, typographical, and prepress services by Creative Services, Inc., Sewanee, Tennessee, 37375
This book is printed on acid-free paper.

The toll on the route to happiness is courage.
  —Abby Vega

Happiness is a journey, not a destination; happiness is to be found along the way, not at the end of the road, for then the journey is over and it's too late. The time for happiness is today, not tomorrow.
  —Paul Dunn

THIS BOOK IS DEDICATED TO OUR DAUGHTER ALEXIS ON HER WEDDING DAY, APRIL 26, 2014.

To my beautiful, intelligent, competitive, and most amazing daughter, Alexis! I love you, Baby Girl, with all my heart. Your happiness, success, and achievements are the exclamation points of my life's plan and my work to break through barriers, tear down walls, remove glass ceilings, open opportunities, and create a better life for the next generation of young women everywhere. You are my soul's inspiration!

I want to start out by apologizing up front for two things. First, I apologize for the times I was absent physically or emotionally for any important event in the past. It was never that I didn't want to be there or that you weren't worth it. I guess in my own way I was trying to do the right things as I viewed the world, creating financial security, providing a beautiful home, an elevated status to launch from, and always making sure that I could care for us both no matter what. My goal was simply to give you a much better life than I ever had. I cannot change how you felt in those moments when you missed me or threw yourself on my suitcase as I was going, saying, "Don't leave me," but know this: I have always loved you, you were always in my heart, and I always wanted the absolute best for you.

I am also sorry that I never let you know why I couldn't let you win at board games or bowling. It was never about beating you (Yeah Right!"). It was important for you to practice losing, to develop the skills necessary to know how to win, like strategy, patience, hard work, and the desire to win. Unlike sports or other life events where unrealistic expectations are set early (because everyone gets to be a winner), there are no trophies or ribbons just for participating in life.

Winning, at life doesn't come easily. There are no guarantees that just because you show up wanting it, that a good life will be waiting for you. Life is what you make it. When you win, it's because you earn it, and even then, you can never stop learning, growing, and challenging yourself to get better, because I guarantee someone else will be working harder than you for the next opportunity to win.

My philosophy for winning is simple. Two words: don't quit! No matter how hard it gets, don't stop trying. When someone tells you "no," don't accept it. It may be "no" for today but it doesn't have to be "no" always. If someone tells you that you are not good enough or smart enough, don't believe it. Anything that you believe possible is more probable if you are willing to work hard enough for it.

Remember that if you work harder, long enough, people will notice you. If you believe in the purpose of something strongly enough, people will follow you. If doing the right thing is your most important thing, even when it's harder to do, your strength and character are what people will remember about you, and these qualities become your legacy. If you truly love and care about people, they will know it and move mountains for you. If you trust that in your heart you are capable of great things, you will be.

Will you win every time? Probably not, but I believe that if you know what losing feels like, it will teach and inspire you to want to win even more.

Do you remember how you felt the first time and place you beat me at Scrabble® and then in a cooking contest? I sure do. The infamous word game win happened in Destin, Florida, and we were on a family vacation, and it was your 16th birthday. The word you spelled to win the game was "quoter." And how about when you beat me at the Cuban pork cook-off blind taste test in my own kitchen? I didn't even get one vote from the judges that day, and I taught you the recipe! Keep those moments safely tucked in your heart, and go to them when you need strength to get through a rough time. It took you 16 years of losing, but you won fair and square both days, and in big ways. I am not proud of my behavior, but I may have even accused you of cheating and bribing the taste judges. That's how much I hate losing! Always treasure those moments, as they represented firsts for me as well for two reasons. First, it was the first time I had lost at Scrabble in a long time, but even more importantly, it was also the first time losing felt better to me than winning, because I knew then that you had learned to play the game!

Working the truck with you those last few months, while planning your wedding and preparing you for your new life with Travis, brought me some of the greatest joy in my life, especially the day we drove around and around in circles in a parking lot at the St. Augustine Pier for the Betty Griffin House 5K event, trying to figure out how to get the serving window on the right side. You laughed hysterically at me, and I got angry because my blondeness and vulnerability were really showing at that moment. I was afraid you'd see I was just an imperfect human and not a super-mom, but it was a perfect day for serving sno-cones on the ocean, and life doesn't get much better than that.

The St. Augustine Pier was also where I wrote my infamous speech for your rehearsal dinner on "How It's Good to Be the King but Even Better to Be the Queen." If you remember, the role of the king is to keep control of the kingdom, protect against enemies, establish the faith, and keep the peace. The role of the queen, on the other hand, is to provide stability, unity, be the face of the monarchy to the rest of the world, and provide heirs to the King and Queen Mother. Therefore, I surmised it was better to be the queen "Because if mamma isn't happy, nobody gets to be happy!"

Your presence, spending time with you, making you laugh—all have made me a better person and mother, even if I am a horrible truck driver. It's the journeys I took that made me happy, not the end spot where I parked.

May your marriage be blessed with true love, honesty, strength, good health, and many, many, years of happiness and, of course, at least one blonde-haired, blue-eyed, dimpled grandchild for me!

Be his wife, his lover, his partner, soulmate, sounding board, and mother of his children, but remember to always be "true" to who you are because your greatest personal joy will always be in your own self love and acceptance and following what you believe, regardless of the pressure from others to think or do otherwise.

Hugs & Kisses,
Mommy

The Family Vega and
Mr. & Mrs. Travis Allen
April 26, 2014

Beautiful Bride ...
Beautiful Venue

CONTENTS

FOREWORD

BY CHRISTOPHER

A MAN WHOSE LIFE WAS CHANGED BY ONE STRATEGIC ACT
OF KINDNESS

WHEN I WAS 20 YEARS OLD, I FOUND MYSELF HOMELESS AND ADDICTED to drugs and alcohol. I left my hometown and traveled over one thousand miles to a long-term drug and alcohol treatment center in South Georgia. I had been there about a month when my 21st birthday rolled around. Naturally, I was very upset and depressed with my situation. It was late August, and I was experiencing heat and humidity like I had never known, being from the Northeast. I remember I had kitchen duty that day, and I was elbow deep in an industrial sink, washing the dishes for the 50+ residents who had just finished lunch, and I was absolutely miserable! I kept thinking to myself, "This is no way to celebrate a 21st birthday." A man walked in the kitchen and said, "Dude, there's an ice cream truck here for you." I looked up at him from the sink and I said, "Shut up, man." He finally convinced me to come outside and look.

Then I walked out into the blazing hot and humid August sun, expecting some sort of cheesy birthday prank, to find—sure enough—that there was an ice cream truck sitting in the driveway! In a haze of shock and heat exhaustion, I met for the first time a woman who I would come to know as the "Kona Ice Lady." Once the initial shock wore off, I was told by this woman that she and her son had traveled 130 miles from Jacksonville, Florida, after my family had asked her to make the trip for my 21st birthday! She asked me if she could come off the truck and give me a birthday hug from my Aunt Sandra. I was speechless, but when she did, we both teared up.

To this day (almost three years later), it is still hard for me to describe how that gesture of love made me feel. After all that I had been through and all that I had done to my family in my addiction, I couldn't believe they had done this

1

for me. It was then that I realized things would be okay, and that my family still loved me no matter what I had done.

I shared a very special moment that day with my friends that I will never forget. I will always remember the day the "Kona-Ice Lady" came to celebrate my birthday with me in the Georgia swamp.

I have worked really hard since then at getting well. I have had both successes and failures along the way, but I finally graduated from the facility and completed a successful transition at the half-way house.

I now work two jobs. My first job is to stay sober every day, because like anything worth having it takes time, dedication, and a daily effort. My second job is at a tractor trailer assembly plant. I would eventually like to go to school for geographical information systems once I can save enough money to get back on my feet.

INTRODUCTION

A ROUTE TO HAPPINESS

WHEN I SAT DOWN TO WRITE THE INTRODUCTION TO THIS BOOK, I CAME across an article written a while back by Bronnie Ware on the topic, "The 5 Top Regrets of the Dying." Since that time, Ware has written her memoir, *The Top Five Regrets of the Dying: A Life Transformed by the Dearly Departing*. While I read the article, it became clear to me that those regrets best expressed the emotions I was feeling when I was finally compelled to make changes in my life that I so desperately wanted but had been too afraid to make for so long. Change is really hard for most people, and I was no exception. If the definition of insanity really is to do the same thing over and over again, expecting different results, then to achieve sanity must mean you have to change things, and sometimes those changes need to be dramatic.

To change things the way I needed for them to change required a lot of courage. So, how do you break a lifetime pattern of bad habits or, like me, successful but bad-for-you habits? And, more importantly, how do you muster the courage to take even that first step?

I won't go into detail about the list of regrets as in Ware's article and book, but you may want to take a look at them and see if any of them resonate with you at this point in your life. I will tell you what I longed for desperately: I didn't want to work so hard for people who didn't appreciate or value what I brought to the table. I didn't want to travel so much and be too tired to exercise and thus be overweight and unhealthy. And I didn't want to be away from my family so often, especially as they were getting older and getting ready to leave me for good. I didn't want to do things that I didn't like or believe in.

I wanted to be able to use all of me—my heart, my hands, my head—not just the part that was suitable for an image I needed to keep at work. I wanted to be able to say what was on my mind and be honest if I felt that someone or something was "full of shit." I didn't want to have to choose between what I was getting paid to do versus what I felt was the most important or right thing to do in any given moment. I wanted to have more fun. Go on adventures. Try lots of new things. Laugh like a child at myself and make others laugh with me and at me. I wanted to work to help more people, not just promote my career. I wanted to sleep. I wanted to play at work. I wanted to be able to make friends, go to a book club meeting and actually have read the book, be a lady that lunched, or simply one who enjoyed being alive every single day.

I wanted to see what it felt like to make money for the pure purpose of giving it away and to test whether I could make little to no money and be happier than I ever imagined. I wanted to know great joy. I wanted to make amends with people I had hurt or had hurt me. I wanted to love with all my heart unashamedly. I wanted to live my life in a way so that at the end, I would have nothing to regret. It wouldn't matter anymore if I failed at things I tried; it would matter more if I simply didn't try.

In its simplicity, *Sno-Cone Diaries* is the summation of my life as a middle-aged woman who—despite "having it all": a great husband, two wonderful children, a successful career, friends, and a beautiful home to go home to—realized that on the inside she was still lost, sad, lonely, and unhappy. The more money I made, the unhappier I became. It was the strangest thing to accept, understand, and process because we live in a society where more is always better, right? In spite of the fifty-plus years I had dedicated to the pursuit of happiness, the American Dream, and the accumulation of wealth, status, cars, and the need to be all things to all people, I felt I had lost my soul. I wasn't being true to myself. I was like a mighty oak tree with blight, tall and strong on the outside but eaten away and hollow on the inside—by years of self-neglect and ignoring that little voice that kept saying, "save me." The emotional pain had started out like a tooth that needed a filling, a dull ache, but left ignored and unattended to for years, it had accelerated into an excruciating pain that had been denied for way too long.

Turning the Big 5-0 was very hard for me on so many levels. I didn't care so much that I was getting older. I cared more that I could feel it in every step, the snap, crackle, and pop in my knees. The arthritis in my hands and hip, the first few painful wobbly steps in the morning until things loosened up, those were only one area of concern. On an emotional level, the pain was even worse. I knew my mother was dying, family relationships were extremely strained over her care, and those both added to the ever present pain in my heart. I'm not even sure if I can describe the pain I was feeling about myself accurately, but hitting a milestone birthday such as fifty will definitely hasten your thinking about certain things and taking an evaluation of who you are, where you are vs. where you want to be, and maybe even asking yourself, "Am I really relevant to anyone? Am I worthwhile? Am I loved in a way that I love others? If I disappeared would anybody notice or care? Is what I have done in my life up to this point made a difference? I've accomplished what I thought I wanted, but have I actually even scratched the surface of God's purpose for me on this earth?"

I remember waking up that beautiful, unseasonably warm, November Sunday morning of my 50th birthday, totally depressed. My sole intention for the day was to sleep it away in an effort to avoid it completely. The kids graciously sang to me and served me breakfast in bed. My mother and daughter Alexis, who came home from college to spend my big day with me, tried desperately to get me out of bed to take me to lunch in the early afternoon, but I was hell bent on being absolutely, dreadfully miserable that day. It was, after all, my birthday, and that was my wish, so I wasn't giving in. Then in the late afternoon, when my husband Juan came home from baseball practice with our son and told me to get dressed, that we were going to meet some friends for a drink, again I dug in my heels. It was my birthday, and I wasn't in the mood to go meet friends for a drink. I had gotten showered and dressed earlier but only into jeans and a tee shirt, and my plan was to go grocery shopping and come right back home. No drinks for me. I had kissed my daughter goodbye and sent her back to college. The day was almost over, and I was convinced that, at my request, no one was going to make a big deal about my birthday, and so it was going to be a day like every other day, something to push through.

To my dismay, Juan insisted on going to the grocery store with me, and amidst an awkward and heated discussion on the short drive to the shopping plaza, he convinced me that we had to go have a drink first with our friends who were waiting for us.

"One drink and then I'm going to get the groceries," I said, as I slammed the car door, not happy with him or in the mood for company. When I looked up at the door to the restaurant, I saw our daughter and son standing there, and then over to the left, our friends sitting on the outside patio, waving to me. Still nothing clicked in my head other than to get this over and done with as quickly as possible, to get back to sulking some more. So you can imagine how I felt when I entered the restaurant and sixty people yelled, "Surprise! Happy Birthday!" I burst into tears and ran for the bathroom.

In all the time I had spent brooding over my life that day, it had not occurred to me even once that I was special and deserving of a surprise party full of friends, great food, presents, and love. It was a very special occasion, and if I were my husband, I would have slapped me silly (verbally) for being such a "Birthday Buzz Killer" all day or even spoiled the surprise just to cheer me up. To his credit, he did neither. He was very proud of himself for pulling off such a perfect surprise and proving that I was foolish to think he would forget such a big day. When Juan tells the story, "I almost fell for her trick about not wanting a big fuss," but thank God he didn't, because I really felt loved that day and maybe even a little bit special—something I hadn't allowed myself to feel in a very long time. Unfortunately, that feeling was short-lived, as my family who lived in Baltimore expressed hurt feelings and resentment that they had not been included.

In fairness to my birth family, they had all been reaching out to Juan to try to offer ideas for my birthday and had even mentioned that I was pretty low, suggesting a surprise birthday party might be a good pick-me-up idea. For many reasons, he rejected their offer of help and planned the party on his own, including only our closest friends in Jacksonville, because he wanted the day to just be about me, without all the family drama, illness, and opposing opinions we were dealing with at the time. If I had had any inkling about the party, I might have done things differently to try to avoid the aftermath, which I have been dealing with for several years now. I'm certain there were hurt feelings amongst my family, but since it was a true "surprise for me," the decision was clearly not mine to make.

In school and in my career, I had always set big goals for myself and was knocking them off like duck pins with 10-pin balls, and yet I still wasn't happy. What else did I need? What else could I do? What promotion could I get? What new job could I be offered? What new house could I buy? I was insatiable in my pursuit of finding that elusive "thing" that would finally make me happy. Sadly, the truth was that each challenge was yet another chance for me to prove to the world, but mostly to myself, that I was worthy of love. I was smart. I was pretty. I was good enough, and I was deserving of happiness. So why could I never feel it?

A dear friend I have known since I was a teenager recently put into perspective the agony that was my heartache when she said, "Honestly, Abby, you are the only one who doesn't look at what you have accomplished and think it's absolutely incredible." Bingo! The light bulb finally went off in my head! I wasn't happy because I wouldn't allow myself to receive the gifts I had been denying myself for years: acceptance of who I was and where I came from, forgiveness for not always being perfect, acknowledgment of my accomplishments in spite of some huge obstacles I had overcome, and believing that I was okay even when what I did or how I did things would never please or gain the approval of certain individuals. I just couldn't see that I was, in fact, loyal, smart, good, kind, caring, successful, loving, giving, hard-working, a go-getter, risk-taker, creative, and, most of all, worthy of my life's blessings and love I had been given. And because of those qualities and efforts, I had made a difference not only in my own life, but in the lives of many I had touched along the way. It dawned on me only then that it was finally OK to give myself permission to be the woman I had always wanted to be.

Until that moment, all I remember is that the happy mask had gotten much harder and heavier to put on each day during my forties. One evening, in an

O'Hare Airport terminal waiting for a flight home, after yet another week away traveling on business, I distinctly remember sliding to the floor. I was in tears, crying for no apparent reason other than my flight was again delayed, and I wanted to be anywhere other than where I was at that moment. Over the next several years, I spent more time alone on the floor at home, in airports, or in hotel rooms, crying and looking for a way to escape.

As odd as it may seem, the perspective you take away when you are looking at things on the floor, curled up in a ball rather than standing proud, straight, and tall, can teach you a lot about yourself if you keep an open mind. One perspective might be, "Well, things just can't get much worse, so I should just "quit this job (marriage, life, etc.)." Another might be, "I kind of like it down here where no one can see me and I can just fade into myself—no one will even notice I'm gone, and I can be invisible." Later, it might be, "I want to get up, but I might need some help (therapy, friends, spirituality), or, "I may be down now, but never, never, count me out. Don't Quit!" I spent time thinking of as many perspectives and explanations for my overwhelming sadness as the numbers of tiles or ugly carpet squares I sat on and wept on before I could make a decision to act.

My sad feelings hadn't happened overnight. They had been building up for years. When I looked in the mirror several months after my first airport meltdown and asked myself truthfully, I couldn't remember the last time I could say that I was happy. See, here is the thing about happiness that I didn't know then: Happiness is, in fact, a personal choice. It's also a daily choice, maybe even a situational choice. I didn't experience or see happiness that often when I was growing up (more on that later), so I'm not sure I ever knew what "happy" looked or felt like. I didn't understand that most people stay stuck in their old patterns and habits. I realized I had been stuck for years, pretending to myself and others that I was confident, content, and always in control, but deep within I was longing to be free to express joy—to laugh, to simplify, to stop carrying the weight of all this responsibility, guilt, and shame, and have silliness, fun, and laughter in my life again.

I wanted the world to know that I was tired and afraid, too, that I didn't always have the answer, or the strength to be the fixer or personal banker for everyone's financial crisis, nor was I the only child of parents who needed care and financial support. I was just one person who desperately needed to feel loved and deeply desired some recognition and appreciation for the good work I was doing. I just wanted to feel like someone was proud of me.

I believe if laughter, fun, and silliness were meant just for kids, God wouldn't have created middle-age. You know that time in your life when you finally arrive at the place where you have always wanted to be, but you can no longer remember where you parked your car, put your keys, or why you wanted to be there in the first place? And, ladies, for us in particular, a sense of humor comes in handy, especially when everything starts falling, lines and creases appear out of nowhere, and we finally stop having our periods, only to be rewarded with spontaneously breaking into personal summers at the most inopportune times.

Juan, my husband, and I started our life together in a good way. We worked, traveled, had movie date nights, bought our first house, and had our beautiful baby girl, Alexis. But just as she came along, our careers started accelerating. My second full-time job, no pay but great benefits in hugs and kisses, other than my first paid job, became keeping track of everyone's schedule and hiring reliable helpers when both of us had to work late or when one or both had to travel. It took Juan seven years to convince me to have a second child, our son Justin, because it was just so hard to manage it all. But thank God I gave in because Justin gives me new life, he has my heart, he loves him some "Momma," he's still ticklish behind his neck even at 19, and he is so "chill" and "knows how to have fun" compared to his momma, papa, and big sis. We took vacations, celebrated birthdays and holidays, but out of 365 days, we spent too few of them just having fun and relaxing. Maybe I'd forgotten how, but I was always so busy working from the earliest age I can remember that maybe I never learned how to have real fun.

I began to imagine how wonderful it would feel to smile, to laugh, to treasure the truly special people—my family and friends—or to touch the hearts of perfect strangers and change the courses of their lives. Somehow, over the years of being more and more successful at my career, I had lost my perspective. I had lost myself. "Fun" needed to be scheduled and had time limits because we always needed to get more things done.

OK, so now that I had achieved this grand revelation about myself, what should I do about it? Was I even in touch with myself enough that I could identify what always made me happy? Did I have the courage to admit to the world what those things were? Would I really allow myself to let go of a six-figure income? What might my husband, friends, and family think of me? Could I withstand the scrutiny, laughter, and ridicule that would surely ensue? Could I really do what I love even if others didn't approve? What would happiness feel like if I actually allowed myself to experience it? Could I let go of the past and truly embrace an unknown and unfamiliar future, hoping to rediscover joy?

I have written this memoir, Sno-Cone Diaries, to share how I changed my life and outline the sweet route to happiness I followed. I am definitely not saying you should choose what I chose. Instead, this book is about encouraging you to decide what your own vision of happiness would look like and map out a route to get it. Naturally, I will understand if your dreams do not include driving a sno-cone truck, writing a book, or being a motivational speaker. My goals are to inspire you to pursue your dreams, ignite your passions, and follow your own path to bliss. If, like me, you have sat on the floor or the bed or the couch and have lost track of what really matters in your life, say, "Hell, Yes! I'm finally going to do what I have always wanted to do, and I will make a tremendous difference in this world!"

I know that by having had the courage to take these risks myself, I don't have any regrets any more, except one: I wish I had done it all sooner!

Blessings on your route to finding happiness!

* * *

Before you read my memoir—pitfalls and all—here's a poem I wrote to myself after my surprise 50th birthday party, as a way of saying "thank you" to all those who made me feel so special. When you read it, you'll have a much better idea of where I was coming from and where I was trying to get to.

I promise if you read my book to the end, in the last chapter I will give you an update on my happiness quotient and where all my adventures have taken me.

Boomer or Bust!
As one of the last boomers to turn 50 this year,
I looked at the challenge with much dread and no cheer.
My goal at 50 was to be fabulous and fit
And know for certain when someone's just full of shit!
She proudly stated, "I'm just fine at 49!
Why do I need to cross over that line?"
And friends told her, "To be wiser and bolder and feel all the love!
And fit in your skin like that hand in a glove.
You think you're the sum of all that you've done?
What you don't realize is your life's just begun!
Because now is the time when it's all about you.
Your blessings are many, and your troubles few.
So dance and celebrate your life with great joy!
Eat that red-velvet cake or get a boy toy!
Look to the past for all that you've learned.
Welcome your future; it's permission you've earned!
To live in the present is really the gift.
Savor each moment and let your heart lift.
For you are amazing, and precious, and rare—
You've given so much to others with resources to spare.

So give yourself, dear friend, what makes your heart sing!
Massages and chocolate, girls' weekends and BLING!!!!
Thank God every day for oceans of grace!
For all the sun damage and still having a face!
For all the lines and wrinkles and skin that just sags,
From years of constant travel and extreme jet lag!
For the honor of joining the AARP!
And let's not forget that first colonoscopy!!!!
For passes allowing you to get out of jail free.
And friends' trips to Jekyll Island to look at dead trees!
For coaches' questions, like, 'What kind of tree would you be?'"
All helped me feel thankful just to be me.
For my trainer who helped me stand straight and tall:
"You want me to do what? AND balance my rear on that ball?"
For Friday night friends from "beach therapy"
Who taught me the joys of red wine as we looked at the sea.
To the ladies who lunch and have coffee and tea
And march to the drumbeat of "Just let it be!"
To new business ventures that succeed or else fail.
And learning to know when it's okay to bail.
For Keith Urban concerts and sea glass collections
And personal shopping trips to help make selections.
For surprise birthday parties that left me in awe!
For funny cards and sweet gifts—all part of the haul.
For nights of no sleep and extreme hot flashes
And the men who still look when I'm shaking my assets.
For a daughter and son who love me no matter
And a husband who still makes my heart go pit-patter.
For brothers and sisters and beloved mom and dad,
Who can make me both unhappy and so damned mad!!
They shared my pains and sorrows and really didn't mind
When nothing but tears could help me unwind.
To forgive and forget and let it all go.
Understanding why "I just need to know."
To all my friends, both old and new,
How'd you put up with me? And not just say, "Phew…!!!!!!!"
Now I want to be happier than I ever could be.
Thank you for truly loving me, helping me see
That older and wiser, we can all understand
Sometimes life's a bitch, and sometimes it's grand!

I love each of you—you've helped me be my best,
Searching to find myself, I've put us all to the test.
I believe I am special: I can more than survive
And finally experience how it feels to be alive!

—Abby Vega
November 15, 2009

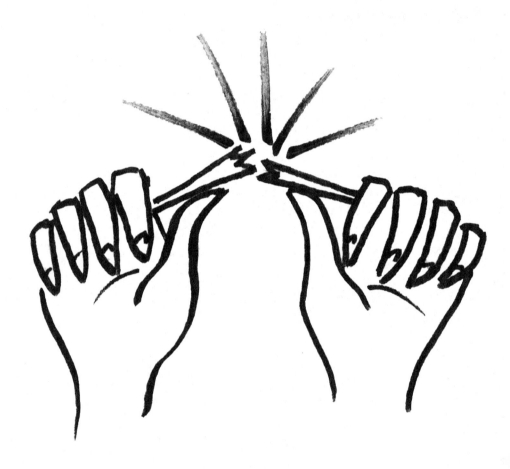

CHAPTER 1

BREAKING POINT

Most people would rather be certain they are miserable than risk being happy.
—Robert Anthony

breaking point (noun). 1: the point at which a person gives way under stress 2: The point at which something becomes critical 3: The point at which something loses force or validity.*

THE INTENSITY OF ENVIRONMENTAL STRESS NECESSARY TO BRING ABOUT A breaking point varies from individual to individual. I was certain that I was miserable. I started having some new health problems. I had gained weight. I felt depressed. I couldn't sleep even with sleep aids. When I finally decided to go to a sleep clinic, hoping for a simple diagnosis of sleep apnea and an Rx for a Star Wars-type-mask, the report indicated something significantly more serious. I arrived at the clinic at 8 p.m. I got wired up from head to toe with monitoring nodes by 9 p.m., and was then told "lights out" at 9:30. For a person who can't sleep in her own bed with feather pillows, down comforter, 400-thread-count sheets, and a perfectly set thermostat, what do you think my chances of falling asleep were while looking like a mad scientist in a test experiment gone wrong? Throw in people staring at me through a glass window, and asking me if I was OK every hour because I wasn't asleep yet. If you said, "Slim to none," you'd be correct. Between 10 p.m. and 6 a.m., the length of the sleep-over party at University of Florida Shands Hospital, apparently I didn't fall asleep until 4 a.m., and in the two hours I slept, I woke up 23 times.

When I met with the doctor for the results, she broke it down very simply for me. After so many years of extensive travel, my circadian rhythm was shot. Her Rx for daytime was a "happy lamp" on my desk with a special bulb that would help trick my brain that I was getting more sunshine in my cubicle (or as I liked

* Merriam-Webster's Collegiate Dictionary, 11th ed.

to call it, "my horse stall," because it was long and narrow with a door but open at the top). Then at night, she said to sit alone in silence in a dark room for two hours before I even attempted to go to sleep to relax and unwind. Neither of these prescriptions was practical for the long term in the fast-paced world I lived in. And the idea of having two hours to waste to sit alone in a room in the darkness to relax, before I tried to go to sleep was nothing short of absurd! Who had two extra hours at the end of the day—considering all I had on my plate—to sit in the dark and relax? The mere thought of that sounded silly to me and just gave me more stress. "Don't you have a pill or something that can help me fix all of this?" I asked.

Looking at me with a face as serious as a doctor delivering a fatal diagnosis, her response was simply: "If you don't change your life soon, you will die." She did not sugarcoat her delivery or mince words.

In my current state, I was on a rapid race to self-destruction.

How could stress and no sleep equal a death sentence?

Little did I know that my drastic lack of sleep had led to fatigue, lack of motivation, and moodiness; reduced my creativity and problem-solving skills; reduced my immunity, which explained my frequent illnesses and weight gain; and increased my risk for heart disease, diabetes, and on and on. At first I went with the easy choice, the happy lamp. My colleagues were certainly intrigued by the new addition to my office decor and after my brief explanation of its function, frequently wore sunglasses as a joke when they came by to see me. While the lamp made for some comic relief, my moods were still more often bad than good. I spent less time with friends and more time alone. On the surface, I was still pretending not to be "miserable" pretty well. The job got done. Bills got paid. Everyone had clean clothes. Groceries got purchased, and Sunday dinner was made. To anyone looking in, we were the epitome of a busy, thriving, everyday American family.

But something just wasn't right within me. I knew I wanted something more, something different, something I couldn't even describe. Yet, I knew that after so many years of working flat out, I still would not have enough courage to say "No" to conventional, logical, traditional, high-paying work if and when it was offered.

However, if you are an intuitive person like I am, one who looks for signs when it comes to making big decisions in your life, you may agree that the incidents that happened right before I started the last two corporate jobs I held were not coincidences. I've been a free agent ever since leaving those jobs.

I had been offered the first of the last two corporate jobs I would hold two days before my 50th birthday. The Saturday evening before I was to start the new job on Monday, my husband Juan and I went out to dinner with several friends to celebrate. I was having a drink and talking with a dear friend when I had the unmistakable feeling that I was going to be sick. I quickly grabbed Juan's arm and told him we had to leave that moment. By the time we drove the 5 minutes to our home, I ran out into the yard and proceeded to be sick for the first of about thirteen times that night. I spent the entire next day in bed. I had never experienced nausea so sudden and so violent in my life. Was it food poisoning? I don't think so because no one else got sick. Yes, I was a little anxious about starting a new job at fifty, but I had been successful everywhere I had worked before. Why did this illness feel so different? My body seemed to be saying, "Please don't do this to me again!" The thought of starting this office job had made me violently ill. Why didn't I listen?

I had worked in many different industries. I had successfully sold everything from non-applicator tampons to million-dollar pieces of surgical equipment. Why did I have this horrible feeling of doom from the day I walked in the door for the interview? Maybe because deep down I knew I didn't want to work for anyone again. I had an entrepreneurial spirit I couldn't shake. I had just spent almost three years developing my first company and was about to sell it. I had accepted the new job in November and told the company I couldn't start until January. Why?

Because my "real plan" was to stall and come up with another entrepreneurial plan. I didn't really want that job. I didn't want to go back to working in corporate America. Alexis and Justin were growing up too fast, and my parents, who lived with us, were aging. My mom was quickly losing her battle with leukemia. Additionally, I knew nothing about the information technology industry I was entering. Despite all my successes to date, I was certain my cover was going to be blown this time because technology without Justin by my side to coach me was a major weakness for me. Why did these feelings of doubt and insecurity continue to plague me, along with the need to achieve more and make more of myself after so much documented success proved otherwise?

Monday morning came too soon, and I was far from feeling 100 percent, but off to work at the new job I went. Later, I found out that my new team members had bet on exactly how long I would last after I asked to go home early that first day because I was still feeling so sick.

PAST

To answer those "why" questions about my compulsion to achieve, my guess is that from the earliest time I can remember as a little girl, several things were always on my mind. First, I sensed that money was a big issue for our family. Some of the earliest examples I can identify are in the ways others looked at my siblings and me, treated us, or spoke to us. Specifically, receiving third-genera-tion, hand-me-down clothes, being called a "beggar kid" when I asked a friend at school to share a treat, and having to go home for lunch when everyone else ate meals at school. We were never encouraged to have any friends outside of our siblings, and if we did have outside friends, they weren't allowed to come into our house. So many people were good and kind and generous to us, giving to our family out of love and concern or maybe pity. I recall whispers, tears, and overheard conversations about "those kids." We always took the help that was offered. But it didn't seem like we could ever pay it back. Maybe we just couldn't. We all knew our poverty was real, even though no one mentioned that word. As siblings, we all carried the shame; no one escaped it. It's how we took it in and processed it that formed the adults we would eventually become.

It's not as if our dad was a bad guy who didn't work. He was an honorably discharged Army veteran. He was also a state employee, a National Guardsman, and part-time weekend grocery store clerk/butcher. But Mom and Dad had six children. Our food, clothing, medical expenses, and school supplies, plus a mortgage payment were just too much for Dad's state salary. On top of all that, add Dad's really bad habit of gambling, and we were never on solid footing for long. I've never figured out what made my father the way he was, but his top priorities then—and even today—are horse racing and his own needs; after those are satisfied, everyone else comes next. I'm not even sure he is aware of it because it's gone on so long, but it's safe to say it took a toll on every one of us, especially on our mother.

Mom would often cry and beg him to stop gambling. I even tried, on multiple occasions as a child, asking him to show his love for mom more, take her out, buy her a gift, surprise her every now and then with flowers, even make her happy by spending more time with us, but all to no avail. "She is always welcome to join me at the track" was his response. My supposition, from the stories he's shared about his childhood, was that this was just how he was raised. He was the 10th of 13 kids, the oldest of the four little ones (how ironic that I am, too). His mom was his father's second wife, and his dad was by no means a "Father Knows Best" model. They lived above a barroom. His father was a barkeep and bookie and had Dad running bets for him before he was old enough to drive. He had a tough life and never learned how to be better.

My mom stayed home to take care of us, cook, clean, and launder endless baskets of dirty clothes. We didn't have a dryer, so she hung our clothes outside to dry on the line strung over our small, cinder block and cement backyard, even in the winter. She worked really hard at taking care of us and making sure we looked clean and nice when we went out in public, setting my sisters' and my hair every Saturday night to have long curls for church on Sunday. We still laugh today about her father being an undertaker. She would often cut the ribbons from flower baskets left at the funeral home to make into bows for our hair. Our fashion label: "We wear dead people."

As a young child, I seemed to have an innate sense of how to make money out of just about anything. I determined if I could make money, I could help. While other girls were dressing Barbie dolls, combing their hair, talking on the phone, learning to paint their nails and toes, putting on makeup, and dreaming of the perfect man, I was down the street on the church parking lot with my two-years-younger sister, using a broom handle, pinky (sponge ball), and glove, playing stickball with a bunch of neighborhood boys, dreaming up ways to beat them at their game, and thinking about how I would make my fortune one day. Even though I was a girl, I sensed that I had to think and play like a man to get the advantage.

So . . . maybe I was a bit odd or quirky as a child, certainly quieter and more introverted than some of my siblings, and maybe because of that a bit needier, maybe a bigger pain in the butt, trying to figure out my place in the pecking order as the true "middle child," number three of six. For me, the designation of middle child always conjures images of the desperate child who is trying to gain attention in any way possible.

I wasn't the firstborn, the first son, or the first daughter. As the story is told, I was born with a head so big that they had to put my mom to sleep and remove me surgically. I didn't get to touch her, be held by her, or bond with her for almost 36 hours. Looking back, I think I've spent my whole life dedicated to Mom, trying to get back those first critical hours I missed. Apparently, the nuns at the hospital where I was born vehemently disapproved of the name my mom had selected for me—Abigail. They thought that was a horrid name for a child and told my mom she should seriously consider something else—until they met me. Then they said, "She looks like an Abigail!" What the hell was that supposed to mean? The origin of the name is Hebrew and means "gives joy." Over time, it seemed liked it was an inauspicious foreboding of my future role in the family: Abby gives joy, but she doesn't take any for herself.

I didn't walk first, talk first, or learn to tie my shoes or ride a bike first. Heck, I wasn't even the first college graduate. It seemed to me that everything I did was old news by the time I figured out how to do it. I guess the most important role I got to play in our family was being the "oldest of the four little ones" (just like my dad), and I took that role very seriously.

For the sake of the story, let's define my "oddness" as I imagine my older siblings may have. Let's start with the first example, which I am not particularly proud of, sticking that very same big, fat head that had gotten me in trouble at birth into a metal casserole dish holder, like a crown. I jammed it onto my head really hard so it wouldn't slip off while I was trying to walk like a princess. Well, it stayed on so tightly that my uncle showed up with a hacksaw, as did the fire department with an axe, to help get it off. Royalty and a princess's life were most definitely not in my future.

Requesting a printing press, sometime between the ages of six to eight, as my dream Christmas present may also have made people scratch their heads about me. Want to know what I was most interested in printing? If you guessed "money," you would be correct. Know what I did with that money I printed? Set up a store. Want to know why? To make more money! I always laughed at the reference "The Beverly Hillbillies" made to their in-ground swimming pool as a cement pond because I personally flourished within the four walls of cinderblock that constituted our cement backyard.

In Baltimore when I was growing up in the '60s, there were little grocery stores on just about every corner, where you could buy canned goods, bread, milk, fruit, ice cream, and candy. As Mom emptied cans, pasta and cereal boxes, milk cartons, soap bottles, and so on, the empty containers became items in my compact, neatly stocked store. My customers consisted exclusively of my younger brother and sisters and Sandy, our cocker spaniel. To run a store, four things were mandatory: inventory, currency, customers, and a cash register. Add cash register to printing press, and you get an idea why "odd" or "entrepreneurial" might be words to best describe how my little mind worked.

So there we were—my sister two years younger, my brother five years younger, and the dog, standing on the back deck of our cherry red, banged up, well worn, hand-me-down Radio Flyer tricycles, complete with a few remaining haggard red and white tassels and their obligatory chrome bells, pushing the two steps it took to cover the distance of my rectangular center of commerce. Our baby sister, eight years younger than I, was too young to play with us then.

Even the lowly position as the oldest of the four little ones came with some privileges: primarily, getting to be the owner, manager, clerk, and cashier. It was my store, after all, and I deemed myself management material even then. When that didn't satisfy me anymore, to generate more revenue, I became law enforcement and handed out tickets to my siblings when they pedaled too fast or crashed into walls or into my store. It was great fun and good practice for the future roles I would play.

But then, a whole new world opened up to me at age eight, when I was finally granted permission to cross the street by myself. Bye-bye cement backyard—hello world! Before long, I had developed a list of customers who called me daily after school, handed me their lists, and sent me off on errands to pick up a few items at some or all of the neighborhood grocery stores in exchange for some loose pocket change. Voilà! An entrepreneur was born! By the end of a good week,

I may have accumulated a dollar or more, and now I was able to buy myself a treat, save for a bigger treat, or treat my siblings to a treat. The power in earning that money was intoxicating to me, and I believe it set me up for what became my path for the next forty-plus years. From child's play, I learned that hard work generated money. Money gave me power. Power gave me choices, and choices would propel me to freedom!

I really wanted to open a sno-cone stand back then, but there was no financial means to do it or physical space to put it outside the house where I grew up. Between the ages of eight and sixteen, I found multiple ways to make money. In addition to running errands, I worked at the neighborhood church's bingo nights, I babysat, I learned to cook by helping a dear, sweet woman named "Miss Grace" wash dishes, set the table, and prepare and serve meals for the Catholic priests at the rectory near our house. Eventually, I was able to snag a job at the rectory at the ripe old age of twelve, working through eighth-grade summer, nights, and weekends, for as many as 12 hours a day, covering three four-hour shifts for the paltry wage of 75 cents per hour. Whenever possible, I filled out birth certificates or Mass cards. I answered phones and the rectory's door when parishioners posed questions about weekend Mass times, the hungry looked for food, or people needed to set up appointments with the parish priests. When I worked, I didn't have to be at home. When I wasn't home, I experienced a world outside my humble existence, like watching a color TV. I got to see what others had that I didn't, and from an early age, I knew what I wanted and was confident that I was meant to earn and to accumulate more in my life than my family had.

I will not bore you with all the details of my childhood. All of my basic needs were being met with food, clothes, and shelter. So how does a child figure out that she is poor? It's not like someone walked up to me directly and called me a poor kid and gave me money or anything. But all of my siblings were aware and impacted by our situation in one way or another. How we processed the information at that time, who was available to influence or help us, I guess, determined the individuals we'd become and the successes and failures we would ultimately have. I guess over time, all the subtle and not-so-subtle hints for me added up to a psychological discomfort, an obsession, and a vulnerability that would last for a very long time.

One moment I will never forget was watching my mother go nose to nose with Sister Edith on the playground after I had come home at lunchtime crying because Sister had punished a few other children and me by making us kneel on hard, uncooked peas she had sprinkled on the floor while we prayed for forgiveness because we hadn't brought money to school in support of the school's annual May Day fundraiser. May Day, or in Polish, Majówka, pronounced (my´oof ka), as it was celebrated at my school, was every kid's dream: amusement park rides, fried dough, cotton candy, and a day off from school. Dad and Mom had been able to pay our way in the past, but they simply couldn't afford it that year, so there was my mom yelling at Sister Edith, asking her, "Don't you think it's already punishment enough that we can't afford to let the kids go with their friends, and now you had to hand out additional punishment?" I was never prouder of my mom than that day! In case you were wondering, hell no, Sister Edith didn't relent, so we sat Majowka out that year!

Truthfully, for a long time after that incident and another one years later, when the very priest I had served meals to and spent many 12-hour days working for refused to marry Juan and me on a Friday night because "then they'd have to do it for everyone," I practiced what was called "Cafeteria Catholicism." I selected the ecclesiastical rules that worked for me and passed on the others, which is still one step above a "Submarine Catholic," one who emerges only for Mass on Christmas and Easter. Bottom line is I have a strong faith in God—of this you can be sure—but it's people, being the imperfect humans we are, that cause me to lose hope from time to time.

If I were asked to define the feeling I had most often as a child in one word, it would be "shame." Shame by its very definition is a painful emotional feeling of guilt, regret, or sadness that you have because you feel that you have done something wrong in any situation of embarrassment, dishonor, disgrace, inadequacy, or humiliation. A condition of shame may be felt by a person because of others' judgments given via words or treatment regardless of one's own experiences, behavior, or self-awareness.

According to Gershen Kaufman in his book *The Psychology of Shame*, "Shame is important because no other emotion is more disturbing to the self, none more central for the sense of identity. In the context of normal development, shame of any kind is the source of low self-esteem, diminished self-image, poor self-concept, and deficient body-image. Shame itself produces self-doubt and disrupts both security and confidence" (1996, p. xiv).

Interestingly, Merle A. Fossum and Marilyn J. Mason, in their book *Facing Shame*, distinguish the difference between guilt and shame: "While guilt is a painful feeling of regret and responsibility for one's actions, shame is a painful feeling about oneself as a person" (1986, p. 5).

Kevin Cooper, marriage and family therapist, quotes from Kaufman's *Shame: The Power of Caring*: "Shame involves the feeling of being exposed or seen in a diminished sense. . . . Children are especially susceptible to shame because they develop their identity based on others' reactions to them."

For me, shame translated into feelings that I was bad or unworthy. Feeling shame can result in placing unrealistic sanctions upon oneself, provide the greatest of all incentives to work to increase stature, or spur us on to our greatest achievements as human beings. For me, the line in between the good and bad impacts of shame in my life was a fine one.

PRESENT

During the last and most recent time I accepted a new corporate position, something way more tragic and devastating happened. I had taken my dad out to dinner for Veteran's Day. During dinner, my cell phone must have rung; the call had come from Ed, husband of Debbie, a very dear, close friend. When I called the number back, he didn't answer, so I left a message, finished my date with my dad, drove us home, and went to sleep.

The next morning, my phone rang at 7:00 with a call from a friend who said that our mutual friend Debbie had died suddenly. Apparently, she had gone out for a run, which she did every day, collapsed with a heart attack, and died alone on the track at the school where she taught. Debbie was just 53 years old. She was thinner and more physically fit than I could ever hope to be. Sadly, she left behind her husband and two teenage daughters. Debbie and her family had left Jacksonville a few years back for her husband's job, but Jacksonville was the place she called home, where her friends were, and where she wanted to return more than anything. I had just seen her a few weeks before, when she and her husband came to Ponte Vedra (where we live, near Jacksonville), looking for a house. I ran into them at the airport on my way to my final job interview. Deb, Ed, and their daughters were living close to where my new job was going to be based, so we were both excited that we would at least get to see each other more often until they could move back. I was able to have lunch with her that weekend before she returned to Delaware, and I distinctly remember thinking to myself that she looked thinner and not at all well. That was the last time I saw her alive.

The day after receiving the news of her death, I was burdened with grieving her loss, leaving home for a week's worth of intensive, new-hire training, and attending my dear friend's funeral. To say training as a new hire was excruciating for me that week is a complete understatement. I don't know how I made it through orientation, loads of HR paperwork, introductions, role-playing, homework, and strategy sessions on what my vision was going to be as the new divisional vice president of the Southeast. All I remember about training is that by Wednesday, my personal dam finally broke, and I could not function. What the hell was I doing here? I didn't look for this job—they'd found and recruited me! I didn't want to work a job like this anymore. I didn't need the money. I didn't feel like being around people anymore, much less supervising them. I had just lost my best friend, and she never got to live again in the one place where she was happy. What would happen to her girls? What would I do without Deb? How could she die when she was so young, fit, smart, good, and someone I was honored to call my friend? Why her? Why now?

Helping Deb's daughters dress for their mother's viewing was one of the worst days of my life, and I am sure theirs as well. Hundreds of people poured in to pay their respects to this woman who gave her all to her family, her daughters, her elderly mother's care, her students—and her fitness and running. One by one, her former students and their parents waited in line to file by Ed and the girls, pay their respects, and share stories of how much she meant to them and how much she had helped them. Hundreds of people came that night.

She was indeed a special woman, a giver. Even in her death, she gave one last time, as she was an organ donor and gave life to countless people unknown. I believe Deb gave me new life that night as well, because in between my tears I promised her that I would find my happiness and that every time I walked the beaches of Ponte Vedra, I would think of her and smile, knowing I now had a dear friend in heaven to watch over me.

After her death, the holidays came and went in a blur. Work resumed, and the everyday activities of life continued, but the hollowness in my soul just got bigger and bigger. One day I was working from home, taking one conference call after another, until I couldn't take it any longer. I took a break and went to get a bite to eat. When I walked in the door from lunch, I simply announced to Juan, who was also working from home that day, that I had just decided that I was going to quit my job. I had been working there for only six months.

Job satisfaction had become more important to me than ever in the last few years. Early in my career, I had worked seventeen years for one company, five years for the next one, two and a half for the next one, and then it got progressively harder and harder for me to stay longer than a year somewhere. My tolerance for office politics, incompetence, lack of respect, mean girls, feeling like I was not making a difference, along with a total absence of morals in the workplace had just worn me out. My husband also knew just how physically sick and emotionally upset I had been after returning from a week-long sales convention for the corporate job I had just decided to quit. So to Juan's credit, having lived with Mrs. Miserable for a long time, he immediately knew that this was serious. He looked at me and said, "OK, Honey, if that makes you happy, go do it."

An hour later, I called the company's HR person and explained everything that had transpired on the convention trip to Las Vegas that had upset me terribly. I shared with him the behaviors I had observed, the words that had been said, and what I had witnessed first-hand: Part of the official training appeared to me to be an unacceptable, culturally questionable way to speak to employees, treat customers, and run a business. Observing such repugnant actions had made me violently ill for the duration of the convention. And then I told him I was done. Of course, nothing is ever that easy or fast because I was completely honest and open about the things I'd witnessed and heard. This set off fire alarms everywhere, which led to many other conversations, but just like that, I watched myself give up a nice, large, six-figure salary.

Was that an act of courage or stupidity? Or had I raised the white flag to give up, give in, and finally take that leap off into the deep end of insanity? Whatever you want to call it, I had finally reached my breaking point.

For me, leaving this job was a life-altering decision. I wasn't getting any younger. I was 53 at that point. Recruiters were no longer calling me weekly with great new opportunities. And on more than one occasion, I had seen the look in the eyes of an interviewer that said, "I can hire three younger folks for the salary of one of you." Quitting that job after such a short tenure meant that there was probably no going back. Considering how miserable I was, you would think that after I quit, the skies opened with bright sunshine and angels singing, but all I felt was panic and fear. My mind raced between two extreme schools of thought, ranging from, "Girl, you are one badass and a force to be reckoned with!" to, "Girl, you are one crazy-ass bitch!" A case for either statement could easily be made. Any way you looked at it, right or wrong, win or lose, sink or swim, the deed was done, and going back was not an option.

The saddest part for me was that in record time, I had made a great connection with the team I had been assigned, and I felt horrible leaving them after I had just gotten them to believe in me. I've stayed in contact with several through Facebook; all of them have left that company.

Soon, my days of retirement turned into weeks, and weeks turned into months. Yet, I still couldn't bring myself to a happy place. I experienced fabulous moments of joy—especially when our future son-in-law asked me to help him pick out Alexis's engagement ring and to play a huge role in the proposal weekend. But those moments only lasted briefly. What was wrong with me? Why couldn't I get past this? Weren't freedom, retirement, and no more unwanted travel what I had been craving for years? You know what scared me the most? Those were the darkest days I had ever experienced, and I was absolutely terrified that, once again, I had everything I thought I wanted, and I still wasn't happy. I feared that the happiness I'd been yearning for was never going to be possible for me at all in this lifetime.

ME

I have often wondered how I got to be me?
If I had listened to all the experts or even believed the results of my own SAT,
I would be stuck in a world that was unfair and so small;
I would still be quiet and never stand tall.
When other girls my age wanted a baby doll to dress,
I wanted to play store and own and operate my own printing press.
I loved to play baseball with the boys and hit it over the fence
And learn the importance not only of offense but the strategy of defense!
I calculated that money was my ticket out,
So that left no time for fashion, make-up, or even Girl Scouts.
Who did I know that was successful, and what did they do?
Certainly if they could do it, then I must be able to, too!
What could I be good at that would help me pass the test?
I was willing to take chances and work harder than the rest.
Failing would never be my option because I'd learn from every setback
And apply that knowledge and skill to get me right back on track!
When people would tell me I couldn't have, do, or be something,
They didn't know I would give up on nothing.
So here I am today, successful and bright,
My life guided by doing what feels right.
So if anyone asks, "What are the keys to your success?"
"Make the most of what you have—even if you perceive it to be less."
    —Abby, 2009

READER PARTICIPATION & REFLECTION EXERCISES

When you have lost sight of your path, listen for the destination in your heart.
—Katsura Hoshina

You'll find a short "Reader Participation & Reflection Exercises" section at the end of each chapter. I designed the questions and suggestions to help you think about how your experiences may relate to mine. Studies on adult learning show that people participate in learning activities because they want to achieve a goal, they like to learn, or they gain lessons from the interacting with others.

Depending on your own learning style, you might like to write your responses to these questions and suggestions into this book (or a diary), say them out loud, or simply reflect on them silently.

1. A breaking point is a critical moment in a person's life. List one or two defining moments that were breaking points for you.

2. How did you feel in those situations?

3. What did you do, or how did you act?

4. If you had a do-over, what would be different this time?

5. As this is a book about finding happiness, write a silly limerick about what would make you happy. Here's an example:

There once was a lady named Abby
Who felt oh so sad and so crabby.
With her new floating device,
flavored syrup on shaved ice,
Her smile radiates new light—not too shabby!

CHAPTER 2

WHAT DOES HAPPINESS LOOK LIKE?

happy (adjective). 1. feeling or showing pleasure or contentment.[*]

ONE DAY WHEN I WAS SITTING IN MY HOME OFFICE, PLAYING AN OLD CD, listening to one of my favorite Gloria Estefan songs, "I Just Wanna Be Happy," I thought, "What did happiness look and feel like for me?" As children, we are born optimistic, happy, full of trust, and with honesty to speak about what we see and feel as it is happening. We are bright-eyed and hopeful every time we open our eyes from a nap. One adorable infant baby boy I recently had the privilege of caring for would start bouncing wildly in his bouncy chair, smile, and start talking the minute he saw me come into his home. We had a great bond. I clearly made him happy. His happiness, demonstrated with his smiles and giggles upon seeing me, brought me great joy. So what happens to us that turns us into a bunch of grumpy old men and women as we age?

THE ABBY THEORY OF HAPPINESS
AND UNHAPPINESS

I believe we create our own unhappiness by the way we think about ourselves. Therefore, if we change how we think about things and ourselves, we will create our own happiness and be happy. Sounds easy enough to do, so why don't we do it? Here are the main reasons I believe I spent so many years being unhappy:

- Obsessive Distress
- Queen of My Universe
- I Can Forgive, but I Will Never Forget
- My Way or the Highway
- Am I Good Enough?
- At the Fork in the Road
- Sailing through Life in an Ocean Half Full

[*] *New Oxford American Dictionary*, 2005–2011.

You may recognize some or all of these behaviors in yourself. If so, can you think of even one good reason for continuing to create your own unhappiness? I have used my experiences as examples to illustrate where I was and how I was feeling at the lowest points in my life. Later on, you'll see how I discovered what makes me happy, and I hope you'll use what I've learned to take your own first steps.

Obsessive Distress

There was absolutely nothing that I didn't obsess over—things that were within my control and things that were totally out of my control. I obsessed about my job, my career, my kids, my husband, my siblings, and my ailing parents. I obsessed about the people who reported to me and their families and issues. And I was distressed that my physical and mental health were being stretched to their limits. I worried that I couldn't be everywhere every time someone needed me. I worried that while I was good at juggling many balls at once, no one ever received the best of me because I couldn't give 100 percent to any one person or goal. I was giving 150 percent all the time but in increments of 1 or 2 percent at a time.

I suspect that even my parents thought I wasn't the greatest mother to my children because I traveled and worked so much, and Mom and Dad often spent more time with them than I did. But what most people did not know was that from our dual income, Juan and I provided my parents almost free room and board, free cars, free insurance, vacations, and clothing. And we paid my mom to be the kids' nanny. The treatment my mom was getting for her leukemia at the Mayo Clinic in Jacksonville was the best in the world and was extending her life and the quality of her life. Before my parents came to live with us, I had asked and paid for my mom to come and babysit when Juan and I both had to be out of town. Sometimes she would stay for weeks at a time because she told me that being with me and the children made her happier than anyplace else. She had money, a car, made friends, and had a real purpose. She often talked about how much she'd like to move to Ponte Vedra, and so she and my father did when a stranger walked to their door in Baltimore and offered to buy their house just as it was.

Sure, I cared about money. We needed to! We supported our children and my parents for more than 17 years with no help from anyone else. Juan loved both of my parents very much and was willing to give them anything they needed for the help they provided us—the loving care they gave our children.

Keep in mind, my mom's diagnosis of leukemia came shortly after they had moved to Florida. We were there for all her hospital stays, blood transfusions, and doctor visits. Assuming both my parents would eventually have difficulty climbing stairs, we sold that house and custom built a new home, complete with a separate entrance, mother-in-law suite, and handicapped bathroom. Because of that advanced preparation, Mom was able to stay in our home through hospice care until the day before she passed away. I'd finally made the decision to move her to an In-House Hospice Facility, with the help of two of my sisters, because Justin was afraid that his grandmother would die in his house, and that made him afraid to stay in his own home. She died peacefully early the next morning with my two sisters by her side. Juan felt so bad for my dad that he told him he could stay with us instead of moving back to Baltimore, which had been the original plan.

It also made me physically ill to think that my own kids might think I was a bad mom because "not now," "maybe later," or "we'll see" were my usual responses to their questions—just so I could get them to stop asking and go away so I could get back to all my obligations and obsess some more. I wasn't listening and giving my whole self to them or to anyone. I was focused on what I believed needed to be taken care of next.

I couldn't even enjoy moments of brief happiness when I had time with the kids because I worried about when the next bomb would drop that would send me spinning again. I never lived for the joy of the moment. I only worried about when any happiness I might feel would go away. Worrying doesn't stop the bad stuff from happening; it just stops you from enjoying the good.

Obsessing constantly over things I could not control made absolutely not one of these issues easier, better, more achievable, or me feel better. I always felt like I was alone and failing because I just couldn't completely accept that a power far greater than I wanted me to have these experiences for a greater purpose, one still left for me to discover.

Queen of My Universe

I must confess I was a total control freak. I'm getting better all the time (now I'm only a bit of a control freak), but back then, no way. When you do so many things for so many people, it's hard to let go or to delegate because you are sure no one will do anything right, thereby making you "Queen of Your Universe." Queens of their universes, when they are being or acting the role, don't even know they are doing it or that it's their own inner anxiety gone amuck! Irrational thoughts take over our bodies and minds, such as, "I'm going to get fired." Or, "They are going to realize how dumb I really am." Or, "Apparently, I am the worst mother, spouse, and caregiver ever!"

We universal queens also have such unrealistic expectations of ourselves that accepting our own imperfections or failures are never options.

Another behavior I was guilty of at work was changing who I was or what I believed to gain approval or acceptance instead of being myself. Those moments gave me the biggest stomach aches of all. An example of this would be making the mandatory appearances at night, after all-day meetings, to have a drink, shake hands, brown nose, and be seen, when all I wanted to do was go to bed after a long day of listening to lectures or training sessions. I am an introvert by nature. I can only recharge when I have time alone.

I hated ambiguity or no direction. Can't get it done if I don't know what it is! Unless I had free rein to create and do things my own way, I believed that neither the processes nor the results would be good enough. So, of course, I tried to do everything perfectly, mostly by myself, and hesitated to delegate anything but the most menial tasks at work and at home—all of which led to so much work, so little time, and complete physical and mental fatigue. My life virtually became unmanageable because if I let one plate crack, my life would be shattered.

I Can Forgive, but I Will Never Forget

I have a kindergarten schoolmate I still owe a punch in the nose to for tying my beautiful dress to my chair on one of the first days of school, so that when I stood up, the chair crashed loudly, which made the teacher yell at me and all my new classmates laugh at me. This girl was the same kid who called me a beggar child. Who, me?

During this period of my life, I could have handed you a book with every wrong ever done to me for the previous fifty years, including the person who did it and when it happened. For some reason, it was easier for me to keep score and remember all the bad things rather than any of the good things or kindnesses I was blessed to receive.

All I can say is piling up that long a list will make you a very angry individual. The list is a heavy load to carry and puts you on a course for misery and loneliness. Some insults and emotional injuries were legitimate, and I dealt with them appropriately, but I did not need to keep a mental score card of every infraction, hurt feeling, disappointment, unkind word or act. Nurturing such lists only corrodes your heart and soul.

For me, learning to let go of most of that baggage, which was weighing me down, was a terribly hard thing to do. I still carry some useless baggage with me (I won't lie), but at least now it's a size that fits neatly under my seat or in the overhead compartment and doesn't need to get checked for me to fly more freely.

My Way or the Highway

Let's just say I prefer things to be done one way. *My way!* When Alexis was first born, Juan would sometimes offer to give her a bath. He loved his daughter, wanted to spend time with her, was fully capable, but sometimes water would get in her face, and she would cry. She was far from drowning, but then I stopped letting him help bathe her because "I became Queen of the Universe in Bath Giving." So he stopped offering to help, and I followed the same pattern for laundry, grocery shopping, cleaning, and so on. Ladies, we dig our own graves this way and then end up doing everything. I specifically remember an incident when I asked Juan to watch baby Lexi one afternoon while I ran errands, did the grocery shopping, dry cleaner pick-up (all that exciting, fun stuff he was fully capable of doing), when my car phone rang. It was Juan in a panic. "What's the matter?" I said, terrified something had happened to the baby, when out of Juan's mouth came this statement: "I wasn't mentally prepared to watch her for this long." I wanted to kill him, but I couldn't because I had created that dependency!

Am I Good Enough?

Guilty again! Blame it on the middle-child syndrome, but I never quite felt like I measured up to other people I knew. However, I was born with a big imagination and one hell of a competitive gene that will not let me fail once I make my mind up I want to do something.

I owe my older sister Veronica credit for my earning a master's degree. I competed with her the most and lost in almost every area. She was taller, smarter, prettier, more popular, had more boyfriends, but when she made up her mind she was going to college and then grad school, I said to myself, "I can so do that!" I couldn't let her beat me at something that was under my control.

But school was hard for me. In first grade when we were learning to write cursive, for some stupid reason, I could not write the capital letter J. So the teacher thought it'd be a great idea to bring my older sister down from third grade to humiliate me in front of the class to practice my J's. Once again, she was perfect. I was not. The good news is I can now write the letter J—which is good because my husband is Juan and my son Justin! A bit of irony?

Later, when I applied for college, I got a peek at my SAT scores. I knew the mountain would be tall to climb and my choices of where to go would be limited to one or two schools, but I knew in my heart that this was something I just had to do. I graduated on the dean's list and went on to get a master's degree from John's Hopkins University. Good heavens! I can be one stubborn, determined, competitive individual, but that seed of doubt about my intelligence was placed early and was deeply rooted. No matter what I accomplished, the mantra "I am not worthy" stayed with me.

At the Fork in the Road

After what you've read so far, you can see that I was really good when reaching the fork in the road, taking the path called the "hard way"! I believe this one characteristic can particularly work in the short term to make you more miserable; however, if chosen correctly, it makes life easier later. Yes, I could have given up after high school and not ridden a public bus 90 minutes each way to the only college that would take me. And I could have refused to work three jobs to pay for it, but where would I be today? Going to college for a bachelor's degree changed my life forever. It was my ticket out to a world I had only imagined existed. It got me my first real job, a company car, and I was off to the races!

After that, working a full-time day job and going to school at night to earn an MBA wasn't easy. I was promoted, the company moved me to Florida, and I had to fly back and forth to Baltimore for 12 weekends to finish classes, but, by God, I did it all. I even failed my last class, Quantitative Analysis 3, and couldn't graduate as planned because we were required to have a B or higher in all grad classes. You see, they let me transfer a few classes from a school in Florida, and because math is not my strong suit, I saved that class for last. Why punish yourself unnecessarily, I say? Because it was a different school, I'd never taken Quantitative Analysis 1 or 2, so I didn't have a clue as to what the professor was talking about. Again, I could have given up, but that stubborn streak wouldn't let me, so the second time I took the course, I got that B I needed, and the rest is history! A stuffed bear was given to me as a gift to comfort me at the ripe old age of 27, and I have him to this day. His name is "Almost Bear" as a reminder that I almost didn't graduate: because I almost gave up on the one-yard line.

The key for handling this stumbling block, so it will not become a perpetual problem, is to be able to discern which things are just making your life harder and which are hard but good for you and will ultimately make your life better.

Sailing through Life in an Ocean Half Full

Here are a few of my other useless old mantras: "I'll never get that job (or promotion). He'll never ask me out. I can't possibly make it on my own. No one wants to marry me! I'm not pretty enough. Who am I to think I can earn a master's degree? I'm that 'dumb Polack from East Baltimore,' [as I was called by an ex-boyfriend]. Who am I to think I can write a book?" Those are the voices that threatened to keep me in many bad places. To achieve success, we must throw out the self-defeating mantras and take one small step forward and then another. . . .

A famous study, the *General Social Survey* (GSS), which began in 1972, is considered to supply the richest data available to social scientists because it has been conducted every other year since 1994 by the University of Chicago's National Opinion Research Center. The survey[*] suggests these general conclusions about happiness:

- About 50 percent of our happiness is genetically determined.
- Up to an additional 40 percent comes from things that have occurred in our recent pasts.
- This leaves only about 10 percent of happiness that is within our control. [Caution to control freaks everywhere: this is really bad news.]
- It turns out that concentrating your efforts on these three values, your "faith, family, and friendships," are the surest ways to happiness. But the fourth value of "work" is less intuitive and way more controversial for most people.
- What is "meaningful acceptable work" to one person is pure drudgery and a demeaning waste of time to another.

The odds were definitely not stacked in my favor because happiness did not appear to run in my gene pool. Certainly my last two job experiences, coupled with the death of my mother and dear friend Deb, were the opposites of joyful recent past experiences, so if the survey is right, that left me with just a 10 percent chance for happiness within my control. Not good odds, admittedly, but it was something I could grab on to and work with.

THREE THINGS THAT MADE ME HAPPY

One day in May two months after quitting my last job, I stared blindly out of my home office window, watching every minute of my hard-fought and earned retirement pass by like the dreaded "40 minutes on a treadmill." Want to know the secret to never aging? Get on a treadmill—that is where time truly stands still. Suddenly, a silly thought popped into my head. For me, that was a sign of progress! The thought was whether, in 10 seconds or less, I could write three things that made me happy. I decided that the usual things like faith, family, and friendships, as mentioned in the GSS, couldn't count, even though they are and always will be givens for overall happiness in our culture and for me—they were not specific enough for me at that time.

* http://www.norc.org/Research/Projects/Pages/general-social-survey.aspx

I asked myself: What brings a smile to my face, makes my heart skip a beat, takes my breath away, and might help me get my groove back?

My 10-second list:
1. Ice Cream
2. Children
3. Touching Hearts and Bringing Joy!

I did it! I did it fast! I did it easily! And, honest to God, I smiled while I was doing it. Could the answer I'd been looking for have been with me all along? Could such simple things be my solutions to finding what had seemed so complex, distant, and elusive for so long?

PAST

I mentioned earlier in the book that I don't remember being happy very often as a child, but there were a few things that made some days better than others. One of those things was a treasured Sunday-night drive to see the "Moo Cows." Go ahead and laugh. We were a city family of eight, living in a less-than-1,500-square-foot home in Baltimore with one bathroom, no central heat or air conditioning, and only a small concrete backyard. So trips to "The Country" that included seeing cows graze, whose milk miraculously turned into ice cream, were rare and exquisite treats on steamy, hot summer nights. Eight of us would pile into Dad's four-person, 1970 Nash Rambler convertible and ride 30 minutes to Baltimore County, thinking we'd died and gone to heaven. Heaven could be described as simply as 5 to 10 degrees cooler, grass instead of cement, and air that smelled like farms instead of city exhaust fumes. On those nights, we all felt relaxed, special, free, and happy.

The other Baltimore summer treasures—besides a steaming hot pile of crabs smothered in Old Bay, Utz's chips, and Tasty Kakes—were *snowballs!!* On just about every street corner, someone set up a snowball stand and served the delicious, cool treat of shaved ice with flavored syrup. For me, an egg custard snowball with ice cream or marshmallow was as good as life could get. Our neighbor Melvin, an older kid, ran a snowball concession from a hidden alleyway around the corner from where we lived. He was not a popular kid because he was overweight and his plaid pants were too tight and always a bit short. He wore black orthopedic shoes, horn-rimmed glasses, wasn't particularly handsome or athletic, and he liked to pretend to be a symphony conductor, waving his arms as he listened to classical music on the radio. In my mind, though, he was a genius because he was making cool, delicious treats and even cooler ca$h.

Often as an adult, when work got especially stressful or unpleasant, I would daydream about quitting my high-powered job and opening my own snowball (aka sno-cone) stand. I live in Florida, for Pete's sake. The weather is good 90 percent of the time. And I live at the beach. It could work, I would think, and then I'd promise myself to consider it seriously "someday" and go right back to work.

After reliving that dream hundreds of times over the years, I took my list of the three things that made me happy one more step that day. Just for fun, I Googled "The coolest thing in ice cream," and there were the two top hits: a Sno-Cone Truck and a Frozen Yogurt Franchise.

Both of the ideas appealed to me immensely for the same reasons—sweetness delivered in such a positive, child-friendly manner and through their owners' commitments to their customers; the franchises represented happiness, satisfaction, and a give-back mentality. Clearly, they both provided ways to touch many hearts.

I explored both options thoroughly, traveling all the way to California to "Discovery Day" for the yogurt concept, to see it, touch it, feel it, and make sure the people really were what they said they were. I took Alexis along to have another pair of eyes and ears to back me up, and though we ultimately decided to go with the sno-cone truck, it wasn't because we didn't like what we saw or heard about the frozen yogurt franchise. It came down to dollars and cents. With Alexis's large wedding pending, we opted for the less expensive option. The best thing about our trip, though, was that we took time to shop for her wedding gown in Southern California, and I fulfilled another dream of mine, which was to watch my baby girl's face light up when she found the gown of her dreams. We ordered it on the spot. (No one went with me to shop for my wedding dress, saw it, or asked about it, oh, and I had to pay for it myself. That wasn't going to happen to my daughter.)

Later, when I clicked on the link for the sno-cone truck concept, the images that popped right up made me feel that my childhood dream was about to come true—on steroids! The more I read about how the franchise worked, the more I knew I loved it! What harm would it do if, while I was "looking for my next real job," I did some more research on sno-cones?

The Scales of Justice

The scales held by Lady Justice symbolize the measure of a case's support and opposition. They stand for truth and fairness. In the eyes of the law, everyone in our country gets treated fairly and equally. Lady Justice's eyes are covered so all can be treated without bias toward gender, race, looks, religion, country of origin—*or occupation?* OK, so I threw that last one in for me. But what if it were true?

So the next thing I did was make a list of the pros and cons of owning my childhood dream:

Pros	Cons
Unlimited, free sno-cones for life.	Get fatter.
They're for children.	Sugar is bad for kids.
I can give back.	I won't make the same income.
It'll be fun.	People will laugh at me.
It's easy.	So it won't work.
I can touch hearts.	That's ridiculous! With a sno-cone?
I can be my own boss.	I'll never be offered work again in this town.
I can make a difference.	But it's ridiculous; folks will laugh.
I can spend time with my kids.	Oh, great, my mom the truck driver.
I can travel with my husband.	But I can't tell anyone what I do.
I will be free.	Driving a 10,000-pound truck?
I can be at all my son's games.	Please don't humiliate me at school, Mom.

For every reason I could think of to do "it," I could think of ten reasons not to. The truth is, I was so excited and energized about the idea of owning my own sno-cone truck that I could hardly contain myself.

However, I still had to cross over a few big hurdles, and the hardest one: How do I gain the courage and words to tell my husband Juan I want to buy, own, and drive a sno-cone truck?

READER PARTICIPATION & REFLECTION EXERCISES

Whoever is happy will make someone else happy.
—Anne Frank

1. Part of being happy and staying happy is about staying balanced and being aware of what your attitude is in any given moment. If you want to stay balanced, rate your happiness level frequently. If it's not in the 7–10 range, you may need to make some adjustments.
On a scale of 1–10, rate your overall happiness level: ____
If you are between 1 and 5, you may need to take some immediate steps. If you are between 6 and 10, you are on the right track and may just need to modify a few things to improve your happiness levels.

2. Of the seven reasons I outlined for my unhappiness, which ones apply to you now?
Obsessive Distress___ Queen of My Universe___ I Can Forgive, but I Will Never Forget___ My Way or the Highway___ Am I Good Enough?___ At the Fork in the Road___Sailing through Life in an Ocean Half Full___

3. In 10 seconds or less, name 3 things that make you happy:
a.

b.

c.

4. If you take faith, family, and friends off your list, what does the list look like? Try to make the list again, based on things that make you happy in your heart, head, and hands:
  a. heart:

b. head:

c. hands:

5. What would your innermost child—with its passion and desire—tell you to do if the scales of justice took away all possible biases and judgments against you, and told you that you could do anything you wanted at this moment. What would that be?

6. What are the pros (good things in your life that don't fit the above items on your list) and cons (obstacles that come to mind) that are keeping you from following your dream?

Pros:

Cons:

Juan, left, and Justin checking out the Sno-Cone Truck

CHAPTER 3

COURAGE

Once you identify the "B" in your Bliss, the next step is to find the "C" for your Courage.
—Abby Vega

Those who are the happiest are those who do the most for others.
—Booker T. Washington

courage (noun). Courage (also called bravery, bravado or valor) is the choice and willingness to confront agony, pain, danger, uncertainty or intimidation. Physical courage is courage in the face of physical pain, hardship, death or threat of death, while moral courage is the ability to act rightly in the face of popular opposition, shame, scandal, discouragement, or personal loss.[*]

HERE'S WHAT I KNOW ABOUT COURAGE: YOU'LL NEVER KNOW WHETHER you have it if you don't exercise that muscle. I walk 3 miles almost every day, and I lift weights a couple of times a week. I do this to fight the battle of the bulge, aging, and arthritis. I can't lift very heavy weights. I still have chicken wings for arms and turkey legs for thighs. I despise sweating! I wish I could tell you I loved exercising, but it would be an outright lie. I do love walking, though, because when I'm walking, I do my best thinking.

And let me tell you, if the sun is shining, there is no problem I can't resolve on a long walk. I set a goal of finding at least one treasure on the beach, like a shark's tooth, a piece of colored sea glass, a piece of driftwood, or a perfect pink seashell, and if I find a treasure, then I know it's going to be a good day. It's a goal I have set for myself that is impossible to miss, so it's a mental game I play to set the tone for happiness by already achieving a goal that day. My point is that exercising is a necessity to stay

[*] https://en.wikipedia.org/wiki/Courage

41

healthy and mobile, but it's also my indulgence, because I get to clear my head so that I can think outside the box to resolve issues that I might otherwise not resolve. I work all my muscles constantly so that they never atrophy. The same approach that you take to your physical health applies to your moral courage muscles as well.

Many people are way more courageous than I can ever hope to be. I have been truly blessed up to this point and have never been put in a life-or-death situation, faced a horrible illness, had a seriously ill child, gone to war, and so on. I am not saying that I can even remotely compare my life's challenges to any of those situations, but on a day-in, day-out basis, when life's not going how you planned it and you feel miserable, sometimes it takes great courage simply to get out of bed each morning and try to change the way you live.

I do not watch much TV. I often don't know which remote to use, so it never goes on while my husband is traveling for work. I prefer to read or write. On occasion, I will admit to a few guilty Netflix pleasures I indulge in on my iPad. *Scandal* and *House of Cards* are two of my favorites.

In an episode in season three of *House of Cards*, the president and first lady have a rather heated argument about the definition of courage. The first lady argues that standing up for and speaking openly about what you believe in and being willing to sacrifice your life for it define courage. The president, on the other hand, defines courage as "keeping your mouth shut no matter what you are feeling and holding it all together because the stakes are so big," reflecting the "just-do-it mentality." They are both right to a certain degree, but how do you know when to use each tactic?

What Justin Taught Me About Courage

I believe my son Justin's definition of courage best reflects the kind of courage I am talking about in this chapter. On a baseball road trip while he was in high school, we were driving back from Sarasota, and I asked him to give me words for the letters that most accurately spelled out the word "courage" as he perceived it. He said:

C Be *Capable.*

O *Offset* Shortcomings.

U *Understand* Circumstances.

R *Reach* Greatest Potential.

A *Act.*

G *Go* for It All.

E Positive *Effects*. Create positive effects on something/someone besides yourself.

Bottom line—Justin defined courage for me using a baseball metaphor. Imagine a pitcher on the mound, preparing to throw a 90-mph fast ball at you. The batter standing there waiting to hit doesn't know what's coming next and only has a split second to decide how to respond.

Both pitcher and batter experience similar emotions, in that they believe they are *capable* of getting the job done.

They both *offset* their shortcomings with other strengths and capabilities. (Mix up the pitches/choke up on the bat.)

Both *understand* the circumstances—that one will win the battle and one will lose. (Get a hit/strike him out.)

Both are ready to put forth their best efforts so their teams will *reach* their greatest potential. (Throw your best stuff every pitch or swing as hard as you can for a hit, or sacrifice with a bunt to advance a runner).

Both analyze the circumstances they are in to *act* in ways that are clear demonstrations of commitment and belief in themselves and their teams. (Throw something they can hit and rely on fielders, or try and blow it by them, or swing and hit it as hard as they can, or try to get the walk to get on base.)

Both pitcher and batter are willing to *go* for it all.

Both hope to create positive *effects* on their teams' outcomes, as well as on their teammates and families and friends who are watching, even when they know only one can win. That's courage!

Past

Throughout my life, I have tried to exercise courage to do the right thing, even when it was unbelievable, unachievable, or unpopular.

When I was a child, one house on my errand route always made me feel very uncomfortable. Without going into great detail, I'll just say that the man of the house was doing things out of his wife's line of sight that were inappropriate for a child, especially a female child, to see. I didn't even know what it was; I just knew it felt wrong, so I took my older sister with me for backup, and he did it again. Together we found the courage to tell our parents. Our parents believed us and addressed the issue expeditiously, but other family members thought we made up the story.

As a teenager, trying to apply and get accepted to college with mediocre SAT scores and no money to pay for tuition, I felt frustrated, demeaned, and angry. On a college visit, I overheard the advisor tell my mom: "Perhaps you should not waste your money here and just teach Abigail a trade. Here she will only be frustrated and fail." Oh, I was frustrated all right, but only with the implication that I was stupid. I never said a word. I just let that embarrassment and anger fuel my energy to do my best academically, while working the three jobs needed to pay for it. I managed to graduate in four years and make the dean's list. I had an important statement to make. You can call me anything and believe what you want, but never underestimate what I am capable of.

And later, as a successful career woman in sales environments, typically with more men than women, I felt that I wasn't always treated as an equal to my male peers by the company or by my customers. Consistently, over a thirty+ year corporate span, I wasn't always paid the same, given the same raises or bonuses the men were given, and wasn't promoted as promised or given the accolades I deserved. Why? Because I was a woman and a mother, thus not the "primary bread winner for my family" and "could not be as serious about my career" as the men who were my counterparts.

Sometimes I took advantage of those opportunities to have a little fun. Early in my career, I sold feminine hygiene products. One of my customers was a buyer who represented many grocery stores. He was not in the least bit interested in what I had to say about maxi pads, mini pads, or, heaven forbid, tampons! He referred to my products as "be no pads." (Meaning, in his words, there would "be no nookie" when women used these products.) When my company had just launched a super-absorbent technology for a new product that I was trying to show him, he said something like this: "They are all the same, so take them off my desk, and if you don't have anything else to show me, we are done here."

My bonus that quarter was based on gaining new distribution on that new product in my Top Accounts, and this buyer was keeping me from making my goal! So I created a poster board with a mini pad, regular maxi pad, super maxi pad, tampon, and the new technology's super-absorbent pad—all mounted as display pieces. I also carried with me some red-colored water in a jar. When I went to his office the next month to make the same product presentation, I unfurled the poster board of sanitary napkins on his desk along with the jar of red-colored water. I offered to do a live demonstration of the absorbency capabilities of each type of pad. Needless to say, the most prominent red object at his desk was his face. He promised to place an opening order of hundreds of cases of every "sku-stock keeping unit" I had if I would "just put that board away and promise to never bring it back!" Message delivered! Mission accomplished! Bonus made!

Other issues in corporate America had to be handled very carefully and seriously. On more than one occasion, I had to look into the eyes of high-level executives as I described instances of inappropriate behavior, commitments made that were not kept, and in some cases what felt to me like discrimination—all that were happening to me and all backed up with mounds of support data. At each of these meetings, I clearly defined and provided documented examples of various colleagues' behaviors, actions, and words as the "pure bull shit" they were.

Not one time were those conversations pleasant, were they acknowledged to be true, or were plans put into place to right the wrongs. Often, these top executives countered my descriptions of the complaints with some combination of anger, denial, threats, bribes, empty promises, and intimidation tactics. Typically, all of those ploys failed and were immediately followed by the companies' human resources' directors calling me in to plan brisk exit strategies for me, because, of course, I was the problem, not the offenders.

By choosing to speak out and stand up for myself, I placed my head in the mouths of lions at the highest levels. I was never eaten alive, but I was chewed up and spit out as waste. The most valuable lesson I learned from these experiences was how to show courage. They could deny me, retaliate against me, ignore me, and keep things going just as they were, but they couldn't take away my pride and dignity for standing up for what I believed to be right and just—and for trying to make conditions better for all the other women I worked with, as well as the young women in the workplace today. Most of the inappropriate behaviors I experienced early in my career during the '80s and '90s wouldn't happen today because of laws now in place. These laws were enacted because women like me had the courage to speak up. We refused to tolerate the bull shit, reported it when it happened, and dealt with the consequences.

So, in summary, I guess the first lady and the president in *House of Cards* were both right about courage. Sometimes you need to stand up and speak, and other times you work hard to prove your point because the stakes are too high to stand down.

As for defying others' interpretations of my SAT score, I have met only one person who had a slightly lower SAT score than I did, and that was recently. Both of us, despite our poor test-taking ability, went on to have successful careers. My points are these: Do not let anyone define who you are, what you are capable of, what behaviors are acceptable at work, and how you should live your life. Don't be afraid to take risks. And, above all, don't be afraid to do what makes you happy! When you're happy, everyone around you is happier. Demonstrate the courage to take that first step toward your own personal happiness. You deserve it!

Now, shall we get back to the story about how I told my husband I wanted to buy a sno-cone truck? That took real courage!

Recent Past

"You want to do what with what?"

"Saint Juan" does not even begin to give an accurate description of the man I have been blessed to be married to for 27 years. No, he is not perfect, although if you ask him, he will tell you that he is pretty darn close to it. He has just learned in our years together to go with the flow—the flow being, "If it keeps the peace or makes Abby's life easier or happier, I should probably say 'yes' to it—no matter how crazy it appears on the surface."

After all, he had already said 'yes' to allowing his in-laws to move in with us, a situation that started 17 years ago and continued until November 2015, when I moved my dad to an assisted living facility very near our house. Juan said 'yes' to a previous business venture idea I had that put my entire 401(k) money at risk. He said 'yes' to a shy woman who invited him to visit in Florida when he had other girls, skis, mountains, and a hot-tub waiting for him because his voice mail was down that day, and he couldn't bear not to show up without at least leaving me a message to say he had changed his mind. What would it hurt to say 'yes' one more time?

So it was out there on the table—I said I had found this really cool sno-cone truck that had music, lights, paintings of funny characters on it, and was based on the premise of "building a business by giving back to your community." I wanted to take money out of our savings to buy the truck and the franchise. I couldn't stop talking about it.

Every time we discussed it, I was smiling. Through the course of our marriage, I had said countless times that I wished I could open a sno-cone stand in Florida, wear shorts to work, and trade the heels and pearls for sunshine and smiles every day by selling people a cooling, sweet treat. We had daydreamed about many possible places that would be good locations for a stand and how we would leave it to our children after they'd finished working their big, important jobs. So, my idea of buying the truck didn't come as a complete surprise—just a little one.

And then: "My dear, oh by the way, how much is this ice house on wheels going to cost me?"

"Not as much as the last brilliant idea I had or as much as the other idea I'm pursuing; ergo, Juan, this is the least expensive, safest way to make me happy!"

My marketing positioning strategy was brilliant, even if I say so myself! I could work from home when I wanted to, be at all our son's sporting events, have a cash business, be held in high regard in the community for giving back when I worked charity events, and help employ some of our son's friends. I could tinker in the kitchen with flavors, and, most importantly, just the thought of starting this new business made me deliriously happy.

He listened, he questioned, he challenged, he reviewed the business materials with me, and then he encouraged me to do it by saying, "If anybody can make this thing work, it's you, baby!" So off to college I went again.

I am tremendously blessed with a husband who has always been completely supportive of me in everything I have wanted to try or to do. Others, I understand, are not as fortunate.

Whether you are married or not, you should be empowered and encouraged to achieve your purpose here on earth—even if it is to drive a 10,000-pound sno-cone truck for the simple motivation of making people smile.

Men have powerful influences over women, especially their wives or partners. They can lift us up and support us or hold us down and diminish us, but the most important man a woman will ever know is her father. How that relationship was formed and flourished can reasonably predict how you as a woman will feel about who you are, what you are capable of, and whether you are worthy enough for love and the many blessings of life.

Part of being happy and staying happy is fully understanding what has made you unhappy to begin with.

> *Marriage is a covenantal union designed to strengthen the capability of each partner to carry out the plan of God in their lives.*
> —Tony Evans

READER PARTICIPATION & REFLECTION EXERCISES

Do one thing that scares you every day.
—Eleanor Roosevelt

1. How do you define courage?

2. Rate yourself on physical and moral courage in tough situations.

3. If you weren't afraid, what would you be doing right now?

4. What are two things you can do every day to exercise and strengthen those courage muscles?

Chapter 4

Women, Take Responsibility for Your Own Happiness

Above all, be the heroine of your life, not the victim.
—Nora Ephron

Two things that are generally known about women's happiness are both rather disturbing:

- Over the last few decades, women, in comparison with men, have become less happy with their lives.
- As women get older, they get sadder.

These trends were noted in a blog called "What's Happening to Women's Happiness?" posted on Huffington Post.com, written by Marcus Buckingham, a best-selling author and a leading expert in personal strengths. The article says that women used to begin their lives more satisfied than men and gradually became less satisfied with every aspect of their lives as they age. Today, statistics show that women don't even begin their adult lives happier than men. One thing we know for certain, says Buckingham, is that women are much harder on themselves and each other than men are on themselves and other men. Women believe that success flows from "drilling down" and fixing their weaknesses. Most of us truly believe we have countless weaknesses.

In his follow-up blog, "Women's Happiness: What We Know for Certain," Buckingham said, " . . . whenever and wherever the research is done on this subject, the results are always the same: women with no kids are, in general, happier than women with kids." He goes on to say that it turns out those bundles of joy also bring a lot of stress. We still want to be great moms, and we believe that our children give our lives meaning and purpose. However, according to

Buckingham's research, only a tiny minority of women feel that their sole purpose on earth is to raise children. The rest believe their purposes on earth, in addition to motherhood, reach far beyond their own front doors.

The scary thing is that children feel all that stress and sadness no matter how hard their mothers try to mask it. Buckingham cites the University of Chicago's *General Social Survey*: Only 10 percent of the children in the study said the thing they wanted most from their mothers was "more time with them." In contrast, 34 percent said, "I want my mom to be less stressed and tired."

To better understand our stress levels, here are a few questions we might ask ourselves frequently:

- How often do we get to do the things we really love to do?
- How often do we feel invigorated or energized by what we have accomplished, not just dog tired and dreading that we have to wake up and do it all again tomorrow?
- How often do we recognize and celebrate what we have accomplished, not focus on the to-do list that never gets done?

> *The great part of our happiness or misery depends on our disposition and not our circumstances.*
> —Martha Washington

One of my favorite neighbors and authors, Jon Gordon, talks a lot about taking a daily gratitude walk. He believes that if we focus for just a few minutes every day on the good things, the things we are most grateful for in our lives, the things we accomplished that day (not the ones we failed to do), we will be calmer, have a better attitude, face new challenges better, and stay focused on the things that matter most. I take my 4-mile gratitude walk daily, and I find my perspective on life when I begin the walk is dramatically different when I am finished with the walk. The walking calms me, lets me hear my innermost thoughts, revel in God's beauty and power at the beach, and appreciate how truly blessed I am.

I am also very fortunate to live in the same town as Jon and have occasionally run into him on the beach or streets of old Ponte Vedra, doing that very thing, taking a walk. Sometimes we chat for a moment. I told him when I first met him, after a speech and book signing he gave at my church, that after reading his story, "The Shark and the Goldfish," I wanted to do what he did for a living. I am so grateful that Jon, as successful as he is, didn't laugh at me, crush my dream, feel threatened, or discourage me when I told him I had stories to tell from a female's perspective of 30+ years in corporate America. The next time I saw Jon, he asked me what my books would be called, or be about, and I didn't have an answer, so as he thought about it, he yelled a possible title to me from across the street. And he waved and wished me successful writing. From then on, whenever he sees me, he asks how the book is coming along. Jon, thanks for taking time to speak with me, for your kind attitude and encouragement, and for using the perfect approach to my "freshwoman" bravado toward book writing. Whether you know it or not, you have been an inspiration to me as I have followed your huge success.

I recommend to you Jon's books *Soup* and *The Energy Bus*. When I worked as a manager, I used these books to inspire and motivate my teams very successfully.

CHOOSE HAPPINESS

You have to choose for yourself what makes you happy and fulfilled. No one can do this for you. Not your husband, your partner, your children, your girlfriends, or your boss. You alone are responsible for your happiness. Make the decision right now to focus on happiness, and then live it every day, moment by moment. Happiness may not come to you overnight, but if you make it your goal and then take steps to achieve it, it will be there for you.

Start by identifying a single moment in your day that made you genuinely joyful, happy, and fulfilled. Be specific as you go over it in your mind:

- Today I was happy when I …
- It felt good to …
- I accomplished …

That moment and every single one like it, taken together, define who you really are and your own truth.

When you commit your life to being true to yourself, these moments that energize and do not deplete you are where you will find your happiness. Stop trying to be the perfect wife, mother, co-worker, or boss. Perfection can't be accomplished. Instead, honor your truth and work to become the best you.

My truth was that, while I liked being called vice president and liked the pay and status that came with it, I didn't always like the ways I needed to act, the actions I had to take, or the decisions I had to make in that role. I worked for great companies, fine bosses, and had co-workers and direct reports I consider to be some of my best friends. I am grateful for all the training, learning, experiences, places I got to travel to, and financial stability those opportunities provided me. However, when I narrow down my experiences very specifically, the moments that made me happiest in my career were when I achieved success because I exercised creativity and was able to bring out the best in others by touching their hearts, encouraging them to be their best selves so they could accomplish goals even they didn't think were possible.

And I was happiest when I did the right things—no matter how hard they were. Sometimes my greatest accomplishments happened because I admitted my strengths and weaknesses and demonstrated how much I valued what each person had to offer, so that together we could achieve more.

Those same moments apply to your work life, home life, and friendships. Don't be afraid to be a little selfish sometimes and take time to do those things that energize you and to abandon the ones—including people—that are energy zappers.

WHAT ABOUT BALANCE?

Forget it! It's not possible to balance your home and work lives perfectly. Trying to achieve an equal balance will only frustrate you more. Instead, focus on those things that make you happiest. Tilt your life toward them.

Remember my three happiest choices: ice cream, children, and touching hearts.

If you really think about it, owning a sno-cone truck was an absolute genius decision for me! I still worked long hours, sometimes had to get up really early to work weekends, but at the end of each day, I felt happy to be selling sno-cones, my childhood dream job! I got to work side by side with a very dear friend. My best, most loyal customers were all the beautiful children in my neighborhood. I touched hearts by serving every child and adult with a personal greeting, making him or her smile. And for the adults, I helped bring back their child-hood memories by allowing them to play—creating their own, unique flavor combinations. Finally, I was able to multiply those moments exponentially by giving proceeds from sales back to charities all over Jacksonville.

And now, as I plan to become a motivational speaker and writer, my days will be full of creating "moments of truth" for people everywhere I go so they may begin their own routes to happiness.

SAY YES TO LIFE!

As women, we have such a hard time saying "No." Yet, we must train ourselves to say "No" to all the "shoulds" without value and to people who are energy zappers. Instead, we must say "Yes" to now moments, to our real selves, to life, to our truth moments, and to happier lives.

This new attitude is working for me. I not only feel happier, I feel it daily, and friends I have known for a long time tell me that with my decision to pursue this venture, I have become the happiest they have ever known me to be. They tell me, "You just smile all the time." I have endless energy and believe I have become a more interesting person with all my stories of adventure.

My purpose for writing this book is to share my story to help others find their routes to happiness, too! Women, let's support each other's dreams and passions. Please don't whisper behind my or any other woman's back that we are giving up on our true potential if we don't reach for the moon and stars at the same time. Success isn't about being the perfect wife, mother, and career woman. It's about fulfilling your dreams whatever they are, taking risks, growing and developing as a person, achieving success on your own terms, and fulfilling God's purpose for you on this earth.

And one more thing: We all recognize who "the perfect ones" of us are. The woman in the perfect outfit, throwing the perfect party that costs a fortune for a group of 3-year-olds who could care less. The woman with perfect hair, makeup, car, husband, and matching purse and shoes for everything. The perfect mom at her child's school who knows the answer to everything because she stays at home and considers herself a better mom than a working mom could ever hope to be. The perfect mom who won't let her children eat sugar from the "scary sno-cone lady." The one who never got over her membership in the high school mean girls' clique.

Two words of advice for all of us: Be nice! You and I don't know these "perfect" women's stories, and we don't know how the rest of our own stories will play out. The so-called perfect women are trying to do the same things you and I are, raising and supporting their families in the best ways they know how to.

Perfection is a very high standard to maintain for a lifetime. Don't look down on working women, and don't look down on full-time moms. They may very well be the same women you need to help you when things start to be not so perfect for you one day.

PAST

In my thirty-plus years in sales, I was guilty of trying to be that perfect woman much of the time. In my line of work, we were taught how to "dress for success" and how the perfect appearance would help us make the perfect presentation and achieve the perfect sale.

Sometimes that was true, and other times it came back to bite me in a big way. Sometimes the customers I was calling on thought I was overdressed, that anyone with such expensive clothes would not be honest, especially on my first jobs calling on grocery stores. I learned the hard way that it was not practical or safe walking in high heels on those slippery tile floors.

Sometimes I stuck out like a sore thumb because the people in particular workplaces dressed and behaved in more casual, laid-back ways than in my corporation. Some of them wouldn't let me in because, they said, "We know by how you are dressed that you just want to sell us something we probably don't need."

Or, I might be making a call at the same time as another group of competitive salespeople. We all looked perfect, so no one really stood above the fray. Those days were commonly referred to as "cattle calls," where as many as a hundred salespeople showed up at a buying office, dressed neatly and perfectly, men and women alike, and we would wait hopefully to be called to have our 3 minutes in front of a buyer to make our pitch. What we were wearing that day had little to do with success in those cases. The choice of who would be seen could be based on timing, volume, need, a shiny new object, or simply pure dumb luck. All the others went home and waited for the next time and hoped to be chosen then.

And sometimes looking perfect just wasn't practical for what you needed to be doing that day, like the time I was selling a full line of grocery products and the owner of the store I was calling on asked me to walk along with him out of the store so he could do another chore—butcher a cow! Picture me in my perfect skirt, blouse, shoes, and briefcase, standing in a cold slaughter room on a floor so slippery from blood, guts, and Lord only knows what else that it took every ounce of willpower and balance not to throw up or slip and break my neck. I learned a very valuable sales lesson that day: Don't wear nice high heels on "slaughter days." I cried when I had to throw those beautiful shoes into the dumpster behind my apartment building.

Practice makes perfect. The best salespeople know what their customers do, what their schedules are, what kinds of conversations build trust, and what makes them like us well enough, ultimately, to buy from us. Dress to the level of the customer you are calling on. It makes them feel more comfortable. After that one hard lesson, whenever I needed to call on the grocer/butcher, slaughter days or not, I wore a nice warm coat and slacks. And flat-heeled shoes. Not the expensive kind.

Here's another one of my silly poems. Laughing at ourselves is healthy!

Boredom

Boredom started today in Indiana,
Staring out at a cornfield eating a Twizzler and banana.
On the conference table is a bowl of cheese-flavored Chex.
How many more pages in this presenter's Power Point deck?
Boredom is good for something; it can help make you sleep.
But as I lie in my bed, my thoughts go too deep.
That age-old question: what keeps you awake at night?
My brain says change is scary, so it could be fight or flight!
Today in my office, at my computer I stare.
Will it be Word, Excel, or email, I wish this moment to dare?
What is my value, my passion, my worth?
Working, how will I ever discover my purpose on earth?
The sun reflects brightly off the wing of this big plane.
It's hotter than heck outside, and I think we could use some rain.
This trip to Dallas is to judge, write, and review—
Oh good heavens, how many more evaluations am I destined to do?
A different hotel room, another night away.
When will this endless road trip be over for me, I pray?
Tonight I had room service with a burger and some fruit.
Writing this much, less reading it, would seem rather moot.
More often I realize change is hard for me;
Routine is boring, but it helps me to see
What I like and what I don't and what I want to change.
It's funny how changing from boring seems awfully strange
What's going to happen if I fail to address?
Who really cares if I fail to impress?
Do I even know who I want to be?
Boring, just a state of mind—I think I'll just make some tea!

—Abby, August, 21, 2011

READER PARTICIPATION & REFLECTION EXERCISES

Create the highest, grandest vision possible for your life because you become what you believe.
—Oprah Winfrey

1. On a scale of 1–10 how happy are you right now? ____

2. Out of any given week, how many hours do you spend doing things that make you happy? ____

3. What are those things that make you happy?

4. If relationships, children, and money were not considerations or obstacles, what would you like to be doing right now?

5. What is your own truth that you have not yet acted upon?

6. What is one step you can take to shift, lean, or tilt toward a lifestyle that would allow you to live your truth?

New trucks in the warehouse!

CHAPTER 5

KOLLEGE ... WHERE HAPPINESS BEGAN

When you follow your bliss, you put yourself on a kind of track that has been there all the while waiting for you, and the life you ought to be living is the one you are living. When you can see that, you begin to meet people who are in the field of your bliss, and they open the doors to you. I say, follow your bliss and don't be afraid, and doors will open where you didn't know they were going to be. If you follow your bliss, doors will open for you that wouldn't have opened for anyone else.
—Joseph Campbell

HAPPINESS BEGAN FOR ME ON AUGUST 19, 2013, WHEN I ARRIVED IN A SMALL town in the Midwest and started college for the third time in my life.

Many people refer to college as some of the best years of their lives, but the first two times I went to college were not very much fun. Getting to my undergraduate school in a suburb of Baltimore took a 90-minute city bus ride, starting at 6:30 in the morning, followed by classes that ran from 8:00 a.m. until noon on Mondays, Wednesdays, and Fridays, and 8:00 a.m.–11:15 a.m. on Tuesdays and Thursdays, followed by another one-hour bus ride to downtown Baltimore, where I worked in a drugstore from 1:00 p.m. to 9:00 p.m. every afternoon and evening. As you can imagine, I hardly had time to be a scholar, but the tuition had to be paid, and my goal was simply to graduate in four years, get the diploma, and begin "living the dream."

A few years later, when I went to graduate school for a master's degree in business administration, I was a little bit smarter but had to work just as hard because I worked a full-time job during the day and went to school at night. At least my employer provided a company car, so no more long bus rides to school, and I was being reimbursed for the tuition!! Progress indeed!

My third experience with higher education was the riskiest, most expensive education I was ever going to receive. Once again, I pulled a significant amount of money out of a savings account, but this time it was to pursue a childhood dream. Was this a mistake? What was I thinking when I made this decision? The courtesy shuttle picked me up and took me to the hotel, where the other fellow students greeted me—all majoring in shaved ice and fun. The people at this college didn't look any different from the people I had worked with everywhere before. They represented almost every nationality, gender, and economic and educational background. They were people just like me who saw the sno-cone franchise as full of endless possibilities for making money, while delivering smiles and happiness in a cup and giving back to their communities!

Maybe this was wasn't as crazy an idea as I once thought. In our group, we had people who were returning for their second or third trucks, lifelong best friends who chose to start a business together, serial entrepreneurs who owned a variety of businesses and were adding a shaved ice truck to the portfolio, and families in pursuit of the American dream of starting a business venture together. I was a middle-aged woman, a former senior executive in search of her soul, her truth, and her happiness by buying a 10,000-pound truck and majoring in sugar, flavor, and ice.

Slowly, we all piled back onto the shuttle and arrived at our destination—an industrial building that housed the Kona Kollege. The future started here!

You can only imagine the look on my face then when we arrived at an open warehouse full of sno-cone trucks. I have been to the grandest resorts this country and a few other countries have to offer, with their world-renowned golf courses and spas, but none of them took my breath away like arriving at the warehouse did that day. No grand ballroom. No marching band. No traveling Broadway theater troupe or special effects, like making snow fall in a ballroom in Puerto Rico—just a dozen or so sparkly new sno-cone trucks playing loud calypso music, with brightly colored characters surfing across the expanses of the trucks, flashing their headlights as if saying, "Hello!" and waiting eagerly to be united with their new owners. They were beautiful, colorful, magical, and fun. All of us couldn't help but smile.

The first thing we did was run to the trucks and climb aboard. The welcoming committee was pleased and proud to show us all the new bells and whistles that had been added to this year's model. My truck was already in Florida, where I would pick it up after the training, so I climbed aboard someone else's and got to take in the sights, sounds, and flavors like everyone else.

And then the moment we had all waited so long for came. It was the chance to make and sample our first sno-cones from our very own trucks—a magical moment! And, yes, we had to learn the proper technique, correct ice temperature, ideal appearance, and optimum taste for creating the perfect sno-cone. Who knew? They had always tasted heavenly to me any time I ever had one. But these tasted better and looked more enticing than any I had ever had before. The colors of the rainbow were represented by red, blue, purple, green, orange, and yellow. Each possible flavor combination was more intoxicating than the next. Oh, the tough choices among lemon-lime, orange, cherry, watermelon, strawberry, grape, blue-raspberry, or piña-colada! The possibilities of bliss in a cup were endless. The first sno-cone I made was so pretty and perfect that I took a picture of it! I truly felt like a kid again. Happy, free, and at peace with my decision.

From there, lessons became a little more serious, as we talked about mixology, "The Simple Syrup Recipe for the Perfect Sno-Cone," which I liken to the formula for Coke or the Colonel's Secret Spices recipe, and the proper care and feeding of a nearly 10,000-pound truck. We discussed how to put fun back into fundraising, truck driving 101, safety, social media, marketing, pricing, and all the other necessary information to jump-start and run a successful sno-cone business.

We each took a turn driving a truck around the parking lot and practicing how to back it into a parking space. I failed Parking 101, which reminded me of how I had failed my original driving test three times at age 16. With lots of practice, I eventually got the hang of it.

I was so excited that I was one of the lucky owners who received two calls the day the company officially added us to its websites as new franchisees. I hadn't been in business 48 hours, and people were already calling me for my services! The first request was to write a proposal for a huge corporate event to be held in September, and this was already mid-August. We hadn't discussed how to do that yet in our training, but the old business degrees kicked in, and I figured it out. The corporation accepted my proposal without a change or even flinching at the price! And then a second request came in. It was a bit more unusual than the first, and I will describe it in the next chapter in more detail; suffice it to say that my acceptance of the second request changed my life.

The two days of training flew by. Our simple graduation ceremony included a review of the fun moments from the classes. We each pinned our areas officially on the map of the United States. We received a Hawaiian lei from the company founder, and our official sno-cone kollege diplomas, signed by all the people from the corporate office, and then a wish of "Aloha and good luck!"

Most people would begin their sno-cone journeys with a long drive home in their trucks filled with supplies to get them started on the road to success, but since my truck was already in Florida, I went back to the airport with lots of time alone to ponder this new path I had chosen.

It was bold! It was scary! It was most certainly different from anything I had ever done before, and yet it felt so right, so in-line with where I needed to get to, and it seemed to free up a part of me that had been locked in a forgotten closet since I was a little girl. At 54, I was finally going to get to play store for real, and in my store I only had one item to sell: Happiness in a cup!

READER PARTICIPATION & REFLECTION EXERCISES

When you are happy, you enjoy the music. But when you are sad, you understand the lyrics.
—Unknown

1. How do you face fear and self-doubt?
   a. Do you plow forward or withdraw?

   b. What are the voices saying to you that make you act in these ways?

2. Are you ready to take the first steps toward happiness and a better life? Name the first two steps you will take. Beside each one, give yourself a deadline.
   a.

   b.

3. What are your definitions of joy and happiness?

4. Using your five senses, what would that joy/happiness look like, smell like, sound like, feel like, and taste like? (Please be specific.)
   a.

b.

c.

d.

e.

5. Play your favorite type of music or song in your head. What feelings does this sound evoke in your heart?

My first Sno-Cone!

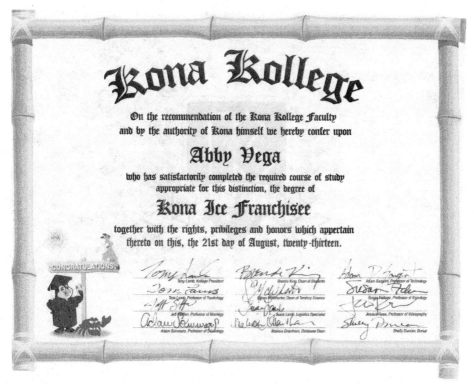

Abby's Kona Kollege Diploma

Abby wearing her penguin head

Chapter 6

Are You Lost?

Bravery is the capacity to perform properly even when scared half to death.
—Former General of the U.S. Army Omar N. Bradley

lost (adjective) 1. Unable to find one's way; not knowing one's whereabouts. 2. Denoting something that has been taken away or cannot be recovered.[*]

I N THE LAST CHAPTER, I MENTIONED THAT I RECEIVED TWO PHONE CALLS while I was still at sno-cone kollege. The first call was a straightforward request for a corporate appreciation event. Could I make 600+ sno-cones within 3 hours? Uh . . . sure, can't everyone? I didn't know if I could or not, but I wasn't about to miss out on this tremendous opportunity, so I said, "Of course" and priced it to win the job. Like everything else I had done in life up to this point, I knew I could figure out how it was going to get done. I am a can-do person, so how hard could it be?

The second phone call was infinitely more interesting than the first one. When I look back, I realize that accepting it changed my life forever. This call came from New Jersey.

When I answered the second call, the first words out of the woman's mouth were, "Please say 'yes' because I've already asked three people, and they all told me 'no.'"

I am a people pleaser and a risk-taker. I wanted to say 'yes,' but I had no earthly idea what she was about to request. She then said, "Please listen, and I will tell you my story, and then I just know you will want to do this for me."

I was intrigued and agreed to hear her out on her special request. She went on to say she lived in New Jersey and had seen similar trucks where she lived, sampled our wares with nieces and nephews at birthday parties, and wanted to book me for her nephew's 21st birthday party. "OK, slow down; are you really

[*] https://www.google.com/?gws_rd=ssl#q=Define+lost

asking me to drive this truck to New Jersey for a birthday party?" Even I couldn't say 'yes' to that request.

"No, no," she said.

"Go on then," I urged her, "Tell me more about this party."

Her nephew was scheduled to arrive soon to live in a place about 130 miles from Jacksonville in Georgia. He would be spending his 21st birthday in a rehab facility. She added that she wanted to send him a message of love, support, and happiness and show him she was very proud of his choice to seek help at last! I was her last chance to make that happen.

Now, the reasons for answering 'no' were many. The location wasn't in my territory. It was 130 miles away. I wasn't properly licensed in my own state of Florida yet, let alone Georgia. It might also be somebody else's territory. And it was a rehab facility, for heaven's sake! Who knows what type of people I would be dealing with? And the kicker: how was I going to price a party for only 30 to 50 people that would take 260 miles of driving, that is, all day to get there, throw the party, and drive back?

I took all the information in, processed it quickly, and without a moment's hesitation, I said, 'yes.' Not only did I say 'yes,' I told her how happy I was to help make her dream come true. *I was going all out with my new endeavor!*

And then I added, "Everyone told you 'no,' but you just hadn't asked the right person yet! I not only sell sno-cones, I bring happiness and joy to others." That would be my mission and purpose for this truck. I said it so confidently and emphatically that no one, including me, would have doubted it to be true. I'm not sure where that confident, bold voice came from. Perhaps it was from somewhere deep inside of me, that place that had been trying for so long to rise to the top and be heard. That same voice that had cried "save me" was now saying inside me, in a magical moment of truth: "My saving grace will be bringing grace and joy to others."

Sandra, the lady from New Jersey, and I agreed on a price and a date ten days into the future, and my new business was launched on day three of owning it. Arriving at home, I was all pumped up and ready to go, but logistically there was still a lot that needed to be done in the warehouse, including cleaning the truck, preparing the syrup, ordering all the necessary supplies, and looking for more business.

Ten days flew by, and the eve of the birthday party day arrived. I was both blessed and cursed to secure a big gig the night before the Georgia birthday party—at the last minute getting a prime location at the biggest rivalry football game in our county. We made a lot of money that night. It was a great test run for what we were capable of doing production wise, and it was nice to see that we quickly became a fan favorite. The down side was we got wiped out of ice, flavors, and had to go extra early in the morning to reload before we could begin our long journey. I had asked our son Justin to go with me for protection, for company, and because he would be turning 16 in one month. He'd get his driver's license soon. I really wanted to give him an upfront, personal view of what life looked like for people who weren't as fortunate as he was and for people who made bad choices.

That day was only the second time I had driven the truck. Yet I was fearlessly confident, and I knew that I was on a mission of pure love and God's work. Justin and I stopped to get ice, loaded up on some snacks, and took a picture of ourselves with the "Happy 21st Birthday, Christopher!" sign in the window to preserve this memory and to let our New Jersey client feel reassured that we were doing what she hired us to do!

The route to the middle of nowhere, our ultimate destination, took us into some places and towns we had never seen before. When we stopped to get gas, people mobbed us, wanting to get sno-cones and commenting on the truck, giving us great ideas of where we should park or go to do business along the way. As a new business owner, I was reassured that what I had been told during training was true: "Just drive it around, and people will come to you." The truck itself would become my best marketing vehicle.

So onward we went on our mission, until we realized that we were definitely not in familiar territory any longer and we'd better start paying attention to the GPS, or we would get lost.

The neighborhoods we were driving in were not only unfamiliar, but they made even an old city girl like me go on high alert. Where in the world could this rehab place be? Everything was old, rundown, beat up, and, quite frankly, scary. The GPS told us where to turn, and then we followed a road toward a one-story facility that was barely marked. The truck's GPS kept 'insisting proudly' (I was already thinking of the truck as a person) that we had arrived at our destination.

My first instinct was to haul ass out of there! The building was at the end of a long, narrow dirt road. Turning around for this newbie truck driver was going to take skill and luck. At the end of the road, where I saw the best opportunity to make a clean break, there was a guy. Dang it! We were spotted! He slowly walked up to the truck and said just three words that described my current situation and exactly how I was feeling in my life. He said, "Are you lost?"

Clearly, the correct answer was 'yes,' but I didn't necessarily want him to know that. And then he said, "Before you leave, can I get one of those sno-cones? We don't get many visitors here." It was one of those 95-degree days with 100-percent humidity on the last day of August in a swamp. How could I say 'no' to his request?

After I put the truck in park and opened the serving window, my heart just took over my whole body, and I told him what my real purpose was and asked for his help. I told him I was looking for Christopher (no last name). He told me they had two Christophers on site. Which one did I want? All I could tell him was he had just arrived and was celebrating his 21st birthday. I also told him if he could help me find Christopher, the sno-cones that day would be free.

He took off running, and in moments there were a dozen or more grown men, ages 21–50, who came running out of the building to see the sno-cone truck. I kept asking every one of them, "Are you Christopher?" They all answered, "No, but he's coming." I asked them all to wait patiently for Christopher to come out, and then there he was right in front of me. Justin was watching this whole scenario unfold with fear in his eyes and his mouth wide open. "Don't just stand there, Justin, we are here to celebrate a birthday! Turn on the lights and music, and let's get this party started!"

I looked directly at Christopher and asked him if he was indeed the birthday boy. Eyeing me warily, he said, "Yes."

"Christopher, I was sent here by your Aunt Sandra all the way from Jacksonville to bring you a message of happiness, pride, and love. She would have loved to be here herself, but since she couldn't, she sent me to wish you a happy 21st birthday! She also wanted me to tell you how much you are loved and how very proud she is of your decision to be here." I then climbed off the truck and hugged him, a complete stranger, very tightly, in the middle of nowhere, and we both started to cry. This was a moment neither one of us would soon forget. I gave him his birthday gift bag with a T-shirt and souvenir cup and said, "You get to go first!"

I then climbed back on the truck and fixed his sno-cone, smiling the biggest smile I had smiled in years.

Each of the grown men from rehab acted like kids at Christmas, as they selected their flavors and then refills. With pure joy, we all danced to the calypso music. I then asked the birthday boy to pose for a picture, holding the head of the sno-cone truck's mascot over his face for me to send back to his aunt. She had instructed me that photos of the men's faces were strictly prohibited for privacy reasons. So I was trying to respect that, yet I knew the moment was special, something his aunt would treasure forever. Not only did Christopher willingly pose for the picture with and without the mascot's head, every one of those men proudly stood in front of the truck, faced the camera, and said, "We are addicts, and we want to do this for you because of what you did for us today."

The party was winding down, and I was getting ready to leave, but the guys were still hanging out by the truck. Of course, a few of them asked me to smuggle them out in my truck. I told them that was against the rules. It just seemed like they didn't want these moments to be over.

And then out of the blue, I got this wild idea to take some of the fallen shaved ice and form it into a ball. I tossed it out gently and hit one of the guys with it. Picture a snowball fight in a Georgia swamp on the last day of August with 30 grown men. Before long, I was handing out snowballs of a different kind, and everyone was laughing and having such a good time. It was one of the most memorable moments of my life. Not only was I not lost, I had found my heart, my soul, and my joy.

In 90 minutes, I was transformed from pure fear and regret to complete and total bliss. I had taken a huge step and was no longer afraid. I was not lost—I was found!

As we climbed aboard the truck to start our long trek home, I faced the same question I had when I first pulled in. How was I going to get it back out? I was still so new at driving the truck that I was having a really hard time turning and backing it up straight. (I had failed that part of sno-cone kollege with three tries.) One of the guys offered to do it for me. I was no longer afraid to trust. So I let one of the strangers in rehab, now a friend, climb into the truck and back it up for me.

As we pulled out of the facility, exhausted from the long drive there and the emotional roller coaster of the event, I looked at Justin and asked him what he thought. He said, "Wow, Mom, that was really something! Thank you for bringing me along! I don't ever want to have to live there, Mom, so I will definitely be good."

"Do you have anything else to say, Justin?"

"Yes, Momma. You crazy, momma, but you crazy good!!!"

READER PARTICIPATION & REFLECTION EXERCISES

Whatever you have experienced in your life is carved in stone. But today, at this moment, you have the power to make the shift from where you are to where you want to be. You are never stuck. . . . You always have choices. You just need to give yourself permission to grow . . . to love . . . to thrive.
—David Ji

1. Name the fear that is holding you back.

2. What is the fear holding you back from doing?

3. How will conquering that fear bring you happiness?

4. When was the last time you completely gave of yourself to someone or something?

  a. What did you do?

  b. How did it make you feel?

5. What scares you the most about finding your happiness?

6. What are the three things you are most afraid of?
   a.

   b.

   c.

7. What are three steps you can take to formulate your plan for finding happiness?
   a.

   b.

   c.

Christopher at his 21st Birthday Party.

Abby and Justin get reasdy to roll out for Christopher's surprise party.

Chapter 7

A Diva Lives in Me

When we step into the unknown, we are free of the past. When we step into the unknown, we are free of every limitation because fresh choices are available in every moment of existence.
—Deepak Chopra

diva (noun). A celebrated female singer; a woman of outstanding talent in the world of opera, and by extension in theater, cinema, and popular music. The meaning of diva is closely related to that of prima donna.*

I AM A NOT A DIVA IN THE TRADITIONAL SENSE OF THE WORD OR BY ANY stretch of anyone's imagination, and if you heard me sing, you would know how far from stardom I am, but after that day Justin and I spent in the swamp at the rehab center, I yearned for more. Not more money, not more things, but more of the feelings I had that day in August. How did I feel that day? I felt free, spontaneous, determined, and in total control of my life. I felt extraordinary—just being me—and that was a great victory. I had conquered a huge fear, that "me" was never enough.

My intention that day had been to find my destination, make sno-cones, and arrive home safely. I had no idea that something so simple and humble would have such a profound impact on three lives, Christopher's, Justin's, and mine. The biggest surprise of all was that in spite of my previous jobs, education, training, award plaques, rings, plus accomplishments, all it took for me to feel extraordinary was to truly be myself. Not the "self" many thought I should be or the one I thought I wanted to be, but the "Real Me," the "Me" that was once described by a co-worker as "Abby Unfiltered."

* https://en.wikipedia.org/wiki/Diva

I would like to borrow this definition of divas from Danielle Schultz, the founder of *School Counselor Blog*,* to describe "Abby Unfiltered":

Divas are
Determined to reach their goals!
Individuals who celebrate their uniqueness!
Victorious in conquering their fears!
Always respectful to others!

Oh, I had seen and felt glimpses of "the diva" before; in fact, I believe "the diva" had been there all along, kicking me in the ass and getting me through my childhood, teen years, college, grad school, and career. How else could I have made it this far? I think we all have inner voices that speak to us and guide us in our daily decision making. Both logic and fear reside in our heads. Sometimes, our heads plays games with us and disguise fears as "rational thinking," giving us a million reasons why we should stay in our comfort zones. Our fears can control us and limit us if we do not face them.

Our hearts hold our intuition, our real selves, and our inner higher selves, the selves that know us totally. It's usually harder to hear our hearts than our minds, but when we practice being quiet and listen to our hearts, we can hear the sound that plays the "music of our hearts."

Don't get me wrong—we need our heads and hearts to make good decisions. There is "wisdom of the head and wisdom of the heart," said Charles Dickens, and let's not disregard the wisdom our guts can tell us. Personal development comes when we learn which one to trust in each situation. For me, thankfully, my heart won, and my life changed from that moment on.

It is my opinion that once you get in the habit of thinking and acting like a diva, the rest comes naturally, including consistently great results. What are some of the habits and behaviors that define a diva?

25 CHARACTERISTICS OF DIVAS

1. Divas know hard work is good for us.
2. Divas always play nice.
3. Divas don't quit.
4. Divas don't bitch or complain—we figure out ways to win.
5. Divas think positive thoughts even if we don't believe them yet.
6. Divas practice random acts of kindness daily.
7. Divas are always gracious.
8. Divas treasure every blessing we've been given.

* http://www.schcounselor.com/2012/05/divas-day-out.html

9. Divas thank God every day.
10. Divas take chances.
11. Divas make our own way.
12. Divas don't let others define us.
13. Divas keep our promises.
14. Divas don't stand on the edge of life; we jump in.
15. Divas say, "I'm sorry" when we are wrong.
16. Divas strive to be what God wants us to be.
17. Divas limit ourselves only by our imaginations and willpower.
18. Divas try new things.
19. Divas believe that we are capable of great things.
20. Divas set goals and achieve them.
21. Divas always give more than we take.
22. Divas help others to achieve success.
23. Divas make mistakes and learn from them.
24. Divas are humble and ask for help.
25. Divas have more fun!

What if we all woke up every morning and set the intention that we would be extraordinary at something that day? Don't think you can do it every day?

I believe you can. We all can: It's not nearly as hard as it sounds.

> **extraordinary** (adjective). Beyond what is usual, regular, or established; . . . remarkable*

To be extraordinary, we have to mix things up in our lives. To be extraordinary, just do one thing differently every day. Start small. Take baby steps. Take the dull, boring things in life that you "have to do" and change them into things you "get to do" or have fun doing.

For example, as the mom, every night my chores include fixing the coffee pot for the next morning and packing my son's lunch. I have been packing lunches for more than twenty years and must have made over a thousand peanut butter, turkey, or ham sandwiches in those years, but having fun doing it? Not so much anymore. Like all good moms, I take pride in providing balanced, healthy lunches with a surprise in every little brown bag, but even that gets old.

So one day, I got this idea that I would have a little fun with Justin by changing up the bag he carried his lunch in every day. At 13, entering high school, you are way past the cool cartoon metal lunch box phase. It's brown bag only. Except that on occasion, my son would misplace his lunch, or someone would steal

* http://www.dictionary.com/browse/extraordinary

it, and I'd get a call from him to please make another trip to the school and bring him another lunch. So I made an executive decision to buy him a thermal bag and wrote on it in permanent marker his last name and phone number. I Know! I Know! So Uncool!! Anyway, that day he came home and told me how he'd almost got beaten up at school because the kids were making fun of him.

"Good heavens, Justin—why?"

"Mom, I am in high school now, and you simply cannot give me a bag with my name and phone number on it." I just looked at him and burst out laughing. From that day on, the challenge for me was to find unique bags or objects to put in his lunch in on a regular basis. Now I say, "So, Justin, what did the kids say about your lunch bag today?"

He just smiles and says he tells his friends it's a "momma thing," and tells them, "It's just how she shows me she loves me and is thinking of me."

From ordinary to extraordinary! Everything becomes more fun when your goal is extraordinary. I could write a whole chapter on what extraordinary has done for my Sunday breakfast pancakes. No more plain buttermilk—we have pearanna, peach, and ravenberry pancakes. All fun and made with so much love.

So, with my sno-cone truck, I decided to try to create extraordinary experiences for the people I served everywhere I went and for me. In the first nine months, I did sno-cone events at the rehab center, football games, pre-game parties, dive-in pool parties and drive-in movies, corporate events, basketball games, farmers' markets, fall festivals, and even a birthday party for Jesus thrown by a family every year in December to collect Christmas gifts for less fortunate children.

I also did a few very special events with dear friends, Elisa and Nando, at the Levy County Learning Academy. This event was called "Operation Sno-Cones & Teddy Bears." The children at this school were high school age, from broken homes or homeless, and some just a step away from prison. For many of them, the only meal they had each day was what they had at school. Not an overly friendly or optimistic bunch of youths due to the circumstances life had handed them. They weren't even allowed to sit close to each other because the school's administrators feared fights or worse.

So you can imagine the initial attitude they had when they were told there was a special treat for them that day right before Christmas. At first, I noticed a lot of rolling eyes as they were told to lineup in single file and approach the truck. I asked each of them his or her name, and then I added that it was my pleasure to serve them and repeated their names. After they got their sno-cones, Elisa, Nando, their son Alex, and Almon Gunter, a motivational coach and guest speaker for that event, handed each one of them a teddy bear, offered a hug, and wished them a very Merry Christmas. Before long, the skepticism turned to joy, and soon these teenagers were playing with their teddy bears, putting them on their shoulders or heads, and had, at least for this one day, a short moment of sweet bliss.

We did a similar event at Baptist Children's Hospital in the spring, where we loaded up red wagons with sno-cones and teddy bears and took them inside because these children were too sick to come outside. One child commented, "This is the best hospital ever" because we delivered the goodies right to their door. I can't even describe the joy I experienced each time I made one of those sick children smile.

The last big event with the sno-cone truck was having it at our daughter Alexis's wedding in April 2014. Hers was the only wedding we had ever done, and I liked it just like that. The wedding was not only the best day of our daughter's life, but without a doubt the best day of my life as well. I never remember being happier than I was that day. That wedding was my victory lap as a race car driver, my walk up to the 18th green with the win in the bag, my super bowl and world series rings put together, Olympic gold medal ceremony, or any of those moments that take a lot of pain, determination, sacrifice, courage, guts, and sheer determination to achieve. Her wedding day and every little nuance about it were a victory dance for my Alexis and me. It was nothing short of a miracle. I had broken the cycle of poverty, broken with tradition, and, of course, broken our bank account in the process, but I would do it all again because people still tell us it was the best wedding they had ever been to. And Juan and I were truly blessed to be able to give it to her with no drama because it was thoughtfully planned, flawlessly executed, fun, blessed by God, and what I believe every girl wants most on that day: It was given out of the truest, purest, and most unconditional love of her parents.

Each event the sno-cone truck made extraordinary was another opportunity for me to learn more about the business, get to meet lots of new people, be creative, bring joy and laughter, and have a great time. I even posted on Facebook that I had finally found the perfect job for me! Being in sales for all those years and facing rejection daily, I felt such relief and joy to have people want my product, come running to get it, throw themselves down in front of my truck and say, "Don't leave!" Or point and drag a parent across a field to come to get a sno-cone.

Most important to me, they'd smile, make a joke, tell me the most amazing things about themselves, and then tell me how great their experience was and how it was "life altering." Or, "You made my day!" Or, "I can now survive another day at work because you've been here!" Or, "Eating this sno-cone brought back the most pleasant memories of my childhood."

People have even called me on my cell phone to ask where I was at that moment because they wanted a sno-cone right then, and they wanted to drive to me to get it. Most of the excitement was the sugar, I presume, but at least a little, I hope, was the experience and me.

At my first corporate event and Sno-Cones and basketball fun.

READER PARTICIPATION & REFLECTION EXERCISES

If you want to know where your heart is, look to where your mind goes when it wanders.
—Anonymous

1. Read the quote above, carry a small notebook, and for a few days write down every thought you have. Thoughts may be about TV, reading, puppies, sex, work, and so on. As your list develops, you will begin to see what topics occupy most of your thoughts. By looking back over your list, you may see how your life is going now or where you wish for it to go.

2. Experts say we need to fill our brains with the things that are most important to us, our goals. List your top 3 goals:

   a.

   b.

   c.

3. What are three Diva behaviors you want to incorporate into your life right now? Today I will try to be extraordinary* at

   a.

   b.

   c.

*Note how people react to your extraordinary changes!

"It's All About the Children"

Birthday Party for Jesus

Chapter 8

Gift of Diamonds

A diamond doesn't start out polished and shining. It once was nothing special, but with enough pressure and time, it becomes spectacular. I am that diamond.
—Solange Nicole

I AM THAT DIAMOND! YOU ARE THAT DIAMOND! SAY IT! BELIEVE IT! AND LIVE it! I believe that diamonds are great symbols for our souls, which lie deep within each of us. Without experiencing hardship, heartache, disappointment, even grief and dismay, we cannot find the courage to live for a greater good. Not even the faith we have in ourselves, in our God, and in the inherent goodness of others will lift us up. If we let ourselves stay like that piece of coal, a rough diamond that remains unpolished and dull, the luster of our individual, extraordinary selves will never appear. I am not the first person to believe that we are all capable of great things, but to tap into that greatness, we have to find ways to be bold and courageous and let ourselves shine.

Here are a few fun facts about diamonds:
- Diamonds are the hardest natural surface on earth.
- Blue and red are the rarest colors, yellow and brown the most common.
- Fewer than 20 percent of the diamonds mined worldwide are of gem quality.
- Only one out of a thousand diamonds weighs more than 1 carat.
- The word "diamond" comes from the Greek word meaning "unbreakable."

THE 4 Cs: COLOR, CLARITY, CUT, AND CARAT

Diamonds are valued according to a grading scale, called the 4 Cs: color, clarity, cut, and carat. A jeweler assesses the value of a diamond by comparing it to a perfect diamond of almost the same size. As diamonds pertain to this discussion, I am going to use the 4 Cs as a metaphor to define how we can polish ourselves up to shine as we were divinely created to be.

Color as it pertains to diamonds means the closer to colorless it is, the more valuable it is. I believe that the more honest, open, and clear you can get with yourself about who you are, what your core values are, what makes you happy, and what you want your life to look like, the more valuable you will become to yourself and others. Why? Because you are revealing your true self, not what others think you are, who you pretend to be, or what others want you to be.

Clarity as it pertains to diamonds refers to the presence of imperfections. The fewer imperfections or flaws it contains, the clearer the diamond. The most perfect diamond would have 100-percent clarity. Get this clear with yourself: we humans are all imperfect. We have flaws. We make mistakes, and we hurt ourselves and others. The closest we can get to perfection is to learn from every experience, not to keep making the same mistakes, to learn to forgive ourselves and others, and to understand that everything happens for a reason, even if we don't know what the reasons are.

Cut means the style or design the cutter used when shaping a diamond for polishing, not its final shape. Cutting creates a diamond's ability to shine and its symmetry, proportion, and polish, which all impact brilliance. If a diamond is cut poorly, it will be less luminous. To cut is to form or shape something. For us humans, there are no shortcuts, easy ways out, or quick fixes to getting to discover who we are and what our purposes in life are. Everything you have done and do in your life adds to your personal growth if you learn to look for the lessons. Each lesson takes us to the next place and, ultimately, to where our destinies reside. Be patient and acknowledge and learn from your life's lessons. Let every cut keep moving you forward to your own brilliance.

Carat is the weight of any gemstone. For our human metaphor, this means we need to strive to improve, to weigh more (YES!) and to become that more-than-1-carat (one in a thousand) individual who is a truly wonderful (not perfect) person, an encouraging mother or father, a supportive daughter or son, a great friend, a valued employee, or an equal partner. Each of us can "gain carat weight" as a person by striving to be better, learn more, take more chances, work smarter, be kinder, help others more often, and stay focused on the path to our true purpose.

Think about this as a mantra:

I am strong!
I am unbreakable!
I am that 1-carat or larger diamond!

Gems

gem (noun) 1. precious stone 2. Something prized especially for great beauty or perfection 3. highly thought of or well-beloved person.*

Now let's talk about the gems among us diamonds. During my year-long journey driving a sno-cone truck, I met some true gems.

By definition, gems make up 20 percent of all diamonds mined because they are considered worthy of gem-quality status. My gems have changed my life forever. They are people who, without even knowing, gave more to me than I can ever repay, other than to acknowledge the gifts they shared and the perspectives they gave me about life, choices, and the little gifts of happiness to treasure each day. The real secret to staying happy is becoming fully aware of these gems and the perspectives they share.

The Policeman. Tall, handsome, smart, brave, and kind. I call him "Officer Friendly." He kept watch over me at a number of events, recommended me for a few more, helped my daughter immensely though a difficult time, kept me company when business was slow, and always purchased a sno-cone, even though I offered it to him free every time. He openly shared the good and bad stories of his career, family, brushes with fame, and hopes for the future. He also scared the crap out of me one night as I was driving the truck back to the warehouse, when he came up behind me, flashing his lights and sounding the siren. He said he wanted to make me feel special, and then he told me my headlight was out, so I needed to drive extra carefully in the dark. I felt so special that I learned how to change a headlight on a truck by myself the very next day! He always knew there was more to my story than just driving my truck. I appreciate his loyalty, respect, interest, bravery, service, protection, generosity, valor, and especially his kindness to my family and me even to this day. May God bless all our men and women in blue!

The Former Addict. I wrote a whole chapter on the one and only experience I had with you, but your aunt has been kind enough to share periodically the details of your journey to wellness. She frequently sends me updated photos of you years later. I am so pleased to see how you have stuck to the program and look so good and healthy. Yours has been a long, tough journey that will have to be fought forever, so I acknowledge your courage, tenacity, and determination to stay well. Thank you for letting me share just a brief moment in your journey. Your story gave me courage to live my story, face my fears and prejudices, and humbled me in my service of others. You taught my son a few things as well

* http://www.thefreedictionary.com/gem

that day. I will always be grateful for that, remember you, and keep you in my prayers. And thank you, Christopher, more than I can express for writing the Foreword to this book!

The Parents. First, I want to acknowledge the parents from the drive-in movie who towed me out of a mud puddle after I got my 10,000-pound truck stuck in it. The mission was about serving sno-cones and raising funds for the school. After I'd accomplished that, the gift you gave back to me was helping me out of the mud, teaming up to rescue me when I was a total nervous wreck, helping me always to remember to bring my boards for leverage in these dicey situations, and always to be open to accepting help when offered. You taught me to believe that we are never alone and that people are genuinely kind and want to help.

To all the other parents who provided the $$ to buy sno-cones, even when you'd rather have given your children a healthier treat, thank you for sharing your beautiful children with me. The part I loved best about selling sno-cones was seeing their smiling faces, watching them dance to the music, feeling the sheer joy and happiness in their eyes when they got their treats, and talking to each one to make him or her smile. Thank you for allowing me to be a small part of their reward for good behavior.

The Children. Each one of you brought the greatest joy to me. I loved our conversations, your loyalty, your creativity, your simplicity, and your passion for life. Thank you for bringing out the kid in me again. To "Pittsburgh," whom I picked on so badly one night because of his choice of football teams to root for; you always came to my window and said, "Remember me"? I could never forget you. You made me smile and laugh and think of my own home team.

And Abby, the little girl I met who told me her name was also Abby, "something we share in common." I gave her a business card to take to school so she could have an important business document with her name on it, too. I just want you to know the highlight of my Mother's Day later that year was when you came to the window calling out, "Abby?" Abby?" When I asked you how you knew my name, you reminded me about the business card and how I'd told you to ask for me by name whenever you saw my truck. Abby taught me that words and intentions are very important, little ears are listening, little eyes are watching, and we impact lives by the example we set and the words we use. Abby reminded me how important it is to keep our promises and remember all the little things.

And the other little Abby who taught me about technology and set up my InstaGram account in 1 minute or less. Thank you for helping me be in the twenty-first century and making something that was so scary to me seem easy.

The Boys with Toys. You are the guys I neighbored with at the warehouse where I kept my truck. I never dreamed I would grow to appreciate ironwork, restored classic cars, and jet propulsion engines, but I can't wait until I get my pearl pink 1959 Chevy Bel Air convertible someday when I am a famous author, so I can show it off to you! What I learned from all of you is that certain men do have great passion for free sno-cones, things of timeless beauty, class, and speed, and at the end of any good day, all roads lead to beer. We all judged each other initially by our covers but learned to respect each other's hard work, results, diversity, and talent.

The Teacher and The Doctor. I already knew the teacher to be just an incredibly beautiful, kind, smart, inspirational 5-carat woman because she taught Alexis in fourth grade and helped to mold her into the smart, determined, and successful young woman she is today. But life happened, and we drifted apart until that Halloween event when she ignored me when I waved at her until I chased her down. How could you have imagined the next time you'd see me I'd be driving a 20-foot sno-cone truck? But you quickly became my biggest fan and cheerleader when I told you what I was doing and why I was doing it. You even got your husband, the doctor, on board to sponsor a few events for charity.

"Operation Sno-Cones & Teddy Bears," Parts 1 and 2, were right up there as diva moments, as we gave Christmas wishes to the kids of the alternative school and pulled red wagons into the hospital for the children too sick to come outside. The children are the reason why I wanted to take this adventure. I wanted to touch as many lives as I could in such a simple way. Together we accomplished that mission, best described by the patient who said, "This is the best hospital ever" when we brought him his sno-cone in bed. The doctor, your husband, had the right Rx for making all those children smile. He's a keeper, and so are you because you believed in me and supported me, and most importantly, you introduced me to the person who convinced me to write this story. I am forever grateful.

The Coach. At the alternative school we visited, there was this guy who came along for the ride because he is a friend of the principal at the school. I had never met anyone so confident, so happy, so passionate, and so darned inquisitive and relentless in his pursuit. He hopped on the truck, introduced himself, made conversation with me, a total stranger, and the next thing I know, he's telling the teacher he just has to talk to me some more. WHY? "What do you want from me?" I asked myself. And there he was again at the hospital event, except this time he insisted on spending time with me on the truck, making sno-cones instead of delivering them to the kids at the hospital. Again, I asked myself WHY? So he told me he had four questions to ask me, and based on how I answered them, the results could change my life. Oh PUHLease!!!!! "Okay," I said, "Ask me your questions because I have an answer for everything."

What he asked me that day and how honestly and openly I answered him shocked the heck out of me. Here I am, telling a complete stranger my life story and asking him why in the world did he want to know all this in the first place? His response shook me to my core. It was like he saw right past the tie-dyed T-shirt, glasses, and the sno-cone façade—and straight into my soul. He told me the stories I had to tell, the accomplishments I had achieved, and the spirit and drive I possessed to overcome any obstacle were similar to those of the greatest leaders in the world.

"Now that's a great pick-up line, I thought to myself," but I still wasn't buying it. He told me, from those four questions I'd answered, I could write at least four books. He said he would be my coach. Okay, so now I get it: "How much will this coaching cost?" He said, "For free." I repeated, "How much money?" Again, he said, "For free." Why?

His response: "Because you'd be cheating the world if you didn't tell your stories." First round winner, The Coach! "Just think about it; here's my card if you want to talk more."

A couple weeks later, I agreed to meet this man, Almon Gunter, and I told him I had no idea how to write a book, so he suggested just do this, and then do this, and then we'll meet again, and I'll tell you what to do next. The next thing I knew, I had a title, a dedication, an outline—and I wrote this book. Game! Set! Match to The Coach! You taught me to trust my instincts, to take risks. You believed in me until I believed in me and helped me to stay "focused to win!"

The Friends and My Family. None of this would have been possible without your support. I know sometimes I am complex and challenging to understand. It's difficult for you to comprehend how I process information and the range of passions and emotions that I have, but while I may seem complex, I am, in fact, very simple. What I need is your unconditional love, support, a few laughs, and the privilege of quality time and conversations with you. That's it! You will never totally understand me, nor I you, because everyone is unique and special, and our life experiences mold who we become. Trust that I always have your best interests as my intentions. I am loyal to a fault, I love you with all my heart, failure is never an option for me, and I am truly blessed to have each and every one of you in my life.

The "Bad Girls." Just three of us girls who found ways to laugh at ourselves and the situations we were in and take dull situations and make them fun. We have at least two or three dinners a year. The three of us had kids in the same class in the high school who became connected through one individual. The year Alexis got married, the other two Bad Girls both got engaged for the second time, while this old fart celebrated twenty-five years of marriage! Guess who got the bachelorette party she'd always wanted? Me! This touched my heart and once again made me feel loved. Thank you, Bad Girls, for being my friends and giving me that moment I'd never had.

The Help. Many people helped me, introduced me to people, did favors for me, and gave me business to get started, but no one helped me more than the Thelma to my Louise, the Lucy to my Ethel, the Laverne to my Shirley. She knows who she is! She has worked with me at several corporate and entrepreneurial ventures. She knows when I call that I won't take 'no' for an answer, and no matter what I ask or how crazy the proposal may be, she pretty much always says 'yes' and goes along for the ride. We take life as one big adventure and turn everything into a game or challenge to be the best. I could not have done any of this without you!! Thank you, Laura, my dear friend, and thank you, sweet Grace, for sharing your Lu Lu with me.

The Recruiter (In Memoriam 1939–2016). I want to thank one other gem, the recruiter who helped me get my first big job, the opportunity that started my career. We met initially over the phone during a screening interview for a job I saw advertised in the paper. I was a little light on experience, sophistication, and savvy, but I more than made up for those with determination. Barb worked her recruiter magic and secured an interview for me, but I did not get the job. Of course, I was devastated and heartbroken when I called her and said, "I can't accept 'no' for an answer; surely there must be something I can do? I want and need that job more than I have ever wanted anything else!" She tried to tell me gently that companies rarely change their minds once they have made a decision. Her only recommendation was to write a letter to the hiring manager and tell him why I was the best candidate for the job, should there be another opportunity or if the situation changed, but she said not to get my hopes up too high.

Lo and behold, two weeks later, I received a phone call saying I had gotten the job! That job launched my 35-year sales career. With that success, Barb and I became fast friends. I would often hang out with her and her husband Paul. Juan bought my engagement ring from Paul.

Barb passed away in January 2016, after a long battle with Alzheimer's. Over the years, we'd touch base every now and then. She and Paul nursed me through a few broken hearts. Barb and Paul traveled from Baltimore to visit me in Jacksonville. They came to our wedding. But life, career, family responsibilities, and living 750 miles apart got in the way of staying close. Last year, when I found out she was sick, I wrote to her several times, thanking her, sharing family photos, and so on. Paul tells me even though she was in her late stages of the disease, when he read my notes to her, she would smile and say, "I always liked her."

Now that you are in heaven, Barb, start looking for a good angel job for me there. I'm sure plenty of good work needs to be done to help all the folks on earth. I love you, my dear friend! Thanks for helping me kick-start a great life and career! Can you please work on keeping me out of trouble here on earth?

The Recruiter

Barbara Langrehr

February 17, 1939–January 8, 2016

READER PARTICIPATION & REFLECTION EXERCISES

There are little gems all around us that can hold glimmers of inspiration.
—Richelle Mead

Look closer at the 4 Cs of your life: Color, Clarity, Cut, and Carat—plus the Gems.

1. Color. How clear is your vision of yourself?
   a. What are your core values?

   b. What do you want your life to look like?

2. Clarity.
   a. What are your greatest strengths?

   b. What are your imperfections?

   c. What help can you ask for to turn those imperfections around?

3. Cut. What are the things you need in your life to position yourself to shine most brilliantly?

4. Carat. On a scale of 1–5 carats, what type of human being are you right now?
at home___
at work___
in faith___
in love__
in friendship___

5. Gems. Which people represent the 20 percent of gems in your life?

Elisa and Ferdinand Formoso with Alex Mairone (center)

CHAPTER 9

LEGACY OF DELIGHT

Carve your name on hearts, not tombstones. A legacy is etched into the minds of others and the stories they share about you.
—Shannon L. Alder

legacy (noun) 1. A gift by will especially of money or other personal property 2. Something transmitted by or received from an ancestor or predecessor from the past.*

delight (noun) 1. A high degree of gratification, also extreme satisfaction 2. Something that gives great pleasure .**

L OOKING BACK ON MY ONE-YEAR JOURNEY OF 7,000 MILES AND 30,000+ sno-cones, I can honestly say that I am delighted with my experiences as well as the results. People define or measure success in so many ways. For some, success means the achievement of a goal. Successful people typically achieve success in everything they do because the foundation upon which their success is built is already there. They have learned from mistakes made in the past. They already know what it feels like to have their hard work and efforts pay off, and the goal they are striving for seems worth the effort. For others, defining success may seem a bit abstract.

Sometimes success means just being the best at what you do—whether it's VP of sales or chief sno-cone technician. Others believe success can best be measured by how valued and appreciated they feel.

Any way you define success, you can be sure that you really are successful if people show some type of jealousy or envy toward you. The more successful you are at being human, the meaner or less friendly some people may be to you. Remember, though, if that happens, rather than feeling sad or bitter toward

* http://www.merriam-webster.com/dictionary/legacy
** http://www.merriam-webster.com/dictionary/delight

93

them, feel secure knowing you are probably doing things pretty well. People are noticing the difference, and you are on the right path. Not everyone will be envious of you or mean, yet sometimes you'll be shocked that some people you assumed loved you and wanted you to succeed will try to undermine you or cut you down to match their views of themselves. Alternately, you'll see that those who truly love you the most are genuinely happy whenever you succeed. Often those people will come as a surprise, like a secret admirer you didn't know you had, and sadly not always the people you may hope or most want them to be, like family or close friends.

I think our definition of success changes as we age. For me, early on it was getting the education; getting ahead; earning awards; and being rewarded with rings, trips, promotions, and titles. None of these are bad things. In fact, they are good ways of demonstrating to yourself and others that your skills are improving and that you as an employee are increasing in value at what you do, as you advance from rookie to superstar in your field.

As I've gotten older, I think more about who I am as a person and how I want to be remembered. I ask myself questions like these: Which people do I make a difference to? What are the stories or memories people will recall when they hear of my passing? Have I inspired others to make good decisions or change their lives? Did I do or say at least one thing that positively impacted their lives or changed an outcome for the better—even if it was as simple as baking them a banana bread when they were down or helping them smile through a bad day? Did I take risks and give chances to people who lacked experience, but who—I knew in my heart—had the fight and fire to win? Have I been the best person I could possibly be as a daughter, wife, mother, and sister? Am I a good, loyal, trustworthy friend? Did I pick you up, make you laugh, or carry you when you were down? Was I a good team player and leader? Did I add value? Did I offer friendship and hope to those who needed it most? Did I put the interests of the team before my own? Did I have your back when I said I did? Did I bring joy and try to make every place I worked a better place?

I am asking myself whether I have any regrets while I still have time to fine-tune my legacy. My list of regrets is quite short now, but there are still one or two that I may have to accept can never be repaired or changed. No one is perfect!

My friends, if you can ask yourselves these questions and be pleased with the answers, you are phenomenally successful at being a human! That's a lot to be proud of, your truest measures of success. You can feel content that your legacy will be one of pure delight.

I Am . . . HOPE

I am the seed of the future on which your life depends.
It is my strength, durability, and flexibility to bend.
The fruit of my vine nourishes your soul.
It is my mission, purpose, and virtue I wish to extol.
I am small in stature but hold such great power
When doubt, despair, and fear envelope you and make you cower.
I am your friend, your comfort, your joy—
The answers lie within you and are yours to employ.
I represent possibility and all that you dream
When vision and action dare to couple and become one team.
I can move mountains and heal a broken heart
If you allow the doubt within you to finally depart.
I go where you go; I never leave your side.
It's how you choose to see things and take your life in stride.
With me anything is possible; you really can cope.
In case you don't recognize me, "Hi, my name is HOPE."
—Abby Vega, June 29, 2011

WHAT HAPPINESS MEANS TO ME NOW

Today happiness is defined for me by these feelings and experiences:

- A toasted croissant; a cup of hazelnut coffee; a sunny beach walk and finding a piece of sea glass; a perfect pink shell; or even a piece of driftwood.
- Being able to do for others and not wanting, needing, or expecting anything in return.
- Not caring about or defining myself by what others think of me or might say about me.
- A level of acceptance and peace that I am who I am, and life is what it is, and both are pretty exceptional.
- A vision when I look back that, in fact, more good than bad happened in my life and that I am truly unique and special because of all those things.
- A level of satisfaction or contentment that I didn't give up what I was aiming for, even as circumstances in my life became difficult. I weathered the storms and became stronger with each new challenge. By responding these ways, I made a difference for myself, my family, my friends, and all those I was blessed to meet along the way.
- I feel blessed with a loving, kind, supportive, and generous husband; two beautiful, smart, healthy children who are close and who love and admire

each other; a great son-in-law; a great support network of friends; and a second chance at a new perspective on life.

- The security of knowing that my family's and my basic needs are met. We live good lives and are flourishing and well-balanced because of our hard work and sacrifices.
- Knowing that I have the power and knowledge to make choices and the strength and conditioning exercises I can practice—like gratitude, joy, hope, and love—that will keep positive emotions high.
- If I breathed not one more breath nor did one more thing, my life has already had great purpose. I touched the hearts and lives of others by giving to them what I so badly wanted for myself: unconditional love, positive reinforcement, acknowledgment, support, kindness, peace, and the challenges to be the very best they could be, no matter what their goals or obstacles were.
- Accepting that, while I may not always realize it and it won't be by everyone, I am genuinely loved and respected by close family, friends, co-workers, and those whose lives I have had the privilege to touch.

READER PARTICIPATION & REFLECTION EXERCISES

I've learned that people will forget what you said, people will forget what you did, but people will never forget how you made them feel.
—Maya Angelou

1. What would you like your legacy to be?

2. What do you think your legacy is now?

3. What are the most important things that must be included as you build the framework of your legacy?

4. Do some research and ask some of the most important people in your life to give you three words to describe your current legacy status.

5. How close are their views to what you want your legacy to be?

"I've got this one—Egg custard for everyone!"

A Cool Treat Before the "I do's"

"Operation Sno-Cones and Teddy Bears" at the Levy County Learning Academy

"Operation Sno-Cones
and Teddy Bears"

"Birds of a Feather Flock
Together—and Eat Sno-Cones"

Easter Sunday Sno-Cones with
Nieces and Nephews

CHAPTER 10

MOVING ON

I had to learn that I knew nothing. I also had to learn that it was okay to think for myself and that my happiness, my true salvation, was not dependent on the approval of others.
—Gregory Michael Brewer

SEVEN YEARS HAVE PASSED SINCE I BEGAN THIS LONG AND ADVENTUROUS road to happiness, as I turned 57 in November. I'd love to tell you it has all been wonderful, but the truth is a lot can happen in seven years. In that time period, I successfully sold my first business, started two new jobs, and quit them both. I raised $250,000 for charity in my first time as a campaign chair while developing the best team I ever worked with and won campaign chairperson of the year. I lost my mother to leukemia and a friend to Alzheimer's; sold a house, moved, and bought a new one; planned and executed the perfect wedding of our only daughter; renewed vows with my husband of 27 years; bought another company; learned to drive a 10,000-pound truck and change its headlight all by myself.

During the process of helping a friend build his wood crafting business, I learned to chalk paint, decorated beautiful trays from reclaimed wood, and assisted in the buildout of a beautiful ladies' clothing boutique in Ponte Vedra. I even tried my hand at car sales, selling 20 cars in 90 days. Not bad for a rookie.

I have reclaimed our home for my husband, our son, and myself as a sanctuary for our mental health, peace, and well-being by finding a beautiful, brand new assisted living facility, just two blocks from our home, for my dad. At 89, he is a fall risk and uses a walker. With our busy schedules and lifestyles, I wanted him to be in a place where all my siblings had access to him whenever they wished to visit, a place where he could receive immediate care if needed in an emergency. He has since given up driving as a condition of receiving a government subsidy benefit for his wartime service.

I've made new friends, lost dear old friends, and written my first book. In terms of jobs, if I don't like doing something anymore, I simply don't do it.

The point of telling you all this is to say that life will always bring with it high points and low points.

The difference for me now, though, is that because of this journey and all of these experiences, I am now much better at handling the peaks and valleys. I am a better balanced, happier, more energetic, and healthier individual because I also lost 35 pounds between January and March 2016, and I am easily maintaining it! And because of this success, I was invited to give my testimonial on live TV[*] about the doctor and the diet program I followed. Thank you, Dr. Thomas,[**] for giving you my 5 minutes of fame and recognition. You rock! Losing weight was a big goal I set for myself in the New Year 2016, along with finally publishing this book. I have more stories I want to tell if people are willing to read them.

validate (verb) 1. To make valid, substantiate, confirm, support the truth of. [***]

approval (noun) 1. The belief that something or someone is good.[****]

OUR NEEDS FOR VALIDATION AND APPROVAL

I will always want to be liked, validated, accepted, and loved. I'm human. Before my intensive soul searching and the sno-cone experience, though, I think the thing I longed for most was approval. I learned that too strong a need for approval destroys your freedom to be who you are. Trust me. I know because I have spent 56 years looking for approval and validation from people who will never give it to me. Waiting for others' approval before we can accept ourselves is a useless waste of our energy and waste of our precious, limited time on earth.

Criticism is something you can easily avoid by saying nothing, doing nothing, and being nothing.
—Aristotle

As I read this quotation from Aristotle and then Sacha Crouch's article, "How to Let Go of the Need for Approval to Start Thriving,"[*****] I learned that early in my childhood I qualified as what Crouch calls a "Need for approval/

* https://www.youtube.com/watch?v=nbv5_e7HkkA
** Jon Thomas D.C DPSC, Director Vibrant Life and Health Center and Nutrimost, Jacksonville; website: DrThomas@VLHCjax.com
*** www.dictionary.com/browse/validate
**** New Oxford American Dictionary
***** http://tinybuddha.com/blog/how-to-let-go-of-the-need-for-approval-to-start-thriving

high performance person," which lasted until just a few years ago. I was a high achiever who always got great results, but at the expense of not doing much that I needed for myself. Now I am working from a different perspective of "Self-acceptance/high performance."

These days, I define and measure success by doing what matters to me most with results that bring me happiness. To reach this point of self-acceptance and understanding, I examined my own father-daughter relationship. I have had to accept that my mom, my siblings, and I were never the biggest priorities in my father's life. After I read Sacha Crouch's book, *De-stress Your Success: Get More of What You Want with Less Time, Stress and Effort*, I was able to analyze the relationship more effectively than ever before, and because of the seventeen years I spent living with him under my roof as an adult, I have come to accept him and love him for who he is.

My dad's loves are horse racing, big band music, and then family. He went to the racetrack almost every day of his life from the time he was old enough to sneak in. He can tell you stories of horses, jockeys, and races he won and lost. He can tell you all the famous people he met at the track, who played or sang in what big band, who the best trumpet player was, or which band leaders excelled best at their craft. He can also tell you every automobile he has ever owned. In contrast, I don't think he could tell you even one of his six children's birthdates. As I came to terms with who he was and is and how I was and am affected by him, I realized that none of us can give what we simply do not have or were never given. I love you anyway, Dad!

One morning as I was leaving to go the warehouse to get the truck for an event, my dad was sitting on the couch. He asked me to come over to him. Shaking his head back and forth in a disapproving tone, he said, "I just never imagined one of my daughters would ever drive a truck!" In that moment, his words cut me to my core. Shaking with anger, I responded as if I were still my little girl self, wanting my daddy to kiss my forehead and tell me he loved me and was so proud of me no matter what. I said, "Yes, Dad, I am the only sno-cone truck driver you'll ever know with a master's degree from Johns Hopkins University!" And out the door I went.

In the past, an encounter like that would've taken me way down for awhile. But I've come to accept that in his heart, in his own way, Dad loves me. He always asked in the mornings who was going with me to help on the truck and what time I would come back home. When I returned, he'd ask how much money I'd made that day. I know he is proud of me: He just doesn't know how to voice it, maybe because no one ever said those kinds of words to him. Juan and I have provided for my dad a great home for the last 17 years. I hear from other people at the facility where he lives now about how much he talks about

me, how proud he is of his grandchildren and me and of our accomplishments. My only "wish upon a star" is that he will find the words to say these things directly to me before it's too late.

I took care of my mom through her illness, provided them relief from financial distress, and gave them two of their ten amazing grandchildren. I couldn't have done or given any more than I have. In addition to being a professional success, I have been an awesome daughter who would make any parent proud.

And after years of struggling to find my own truths, I've finally succeeded as a person, a whole person. I don't need my dad's or anyone else's permission to be the woman I am. Dad, you are my father, and I love you for who you are and for what you have given to me in my lifetime. I am strong-willed, know right from wrong, have a passion and love for music, and an undying spirit that allowed me to turn that piece of coal into the diamond I am today. I also have an uncanny ability to see objects, situations, and individuals in unique ways, including what most people would view as unsalvageable waste material. I have the instincts and abilities to turn those items, circumstances, and people into gems—huge successes. Some of those skills I got from you, Dad.

Do you—as I did for years—hold back from being your true self because you fear disapproval or criticism instead of doing what is valuable, effective, and important to you?

Dear readers, please don't waste another minute of your lives looking for the approval that you may never get. Stop looking for it from your dad, mom, husband, relatives, bosses, friends, and coworkers. Trust that you are smart enough, attractive enough, successful enough. In fact, believe that you are pretty darn awesome just being you!

On April 5, 2014, the *Florida Times Union* contained a front-page article in its Shorelines section: "Have Truck, Will Contribute." The article validated the intent, effort, impact, and contributions I'd made after only eight months in business. Learn to trust that if what you are doing feels right to you and makes you happy, it is probably a good thing with validation enough to be approved by the only person who really matters—You!

In just 11 months of having the sno-cone truck, my life changed. I grew a business from zero to $100,000, gave back a large percentage of sales to my community, wrote the manuscript of this first book, accepted an offer for the purchase of my business that allowed me to put all the money I'd borrowed back into savings, plus nice rewards for my labor of love. I had the pleasure of touching thousands of lives, had great fun, reconnected with dear old friends, made many new friends, grew tremendously as a person, and checked a big box on my bucket list. Nobody got hurt (except for my arthritic hands), and the entire experience has brought out the adventurer in me, so much so that I can't wait to see where I go next. Any way you define success, I believe my story will open your mind to redefining success to include the things that bring you and others the greatest joy.

> *Someday we'll forget the hurt, the reason why we cried, and who caused us pain. We will finally realize that the secret of being free is not revenge, but letting things unfold in their own time. After all, what matters most is not the first but the last chapter of our life, which shows how well we ran the race. So smile, laugh, forgive, forget, believe, and love all over again.*
> —Unknown

READER PARTICIPATION & REFLECTION EXERCISES

The real voyage of discovery consists not in seeking new landscapes but in having new eyes.
—Marcel Proust

1. Greek philosopher Epicurus said, "Happiness is rooted in the elimination of pain and the achievement of tranquility." What are the painful things that must be eliminated from your life to achieve the tranquility you desire?

2. Whose approval are you still waiting to get that keeps you from experiencing joy?

3. Name ten qualities that make you an awesome human being right now.

4. What are three great things you've already accomplished?

5. What are your plans for bringing more happiness into your life?

SUMMARY

Don't fear failure so much that you refuse to try new things. The saddest summary of a life contains three descriptions: could have, might have, and should have.
    —Louis E. Boone

someday (adverb) 1. at some time in the future.[*]

There are 7 days in every week, and one of them isn't called 'Someday.'[**]

WE ALL HAVE SEVEN CHANCES EACH WEEK TO START OFF ON A NEW PATH, a new destiny, a new future, a new adventure, a new you, a new me. "Someday," if you let it, becomes never.

Every day on this earth is precious, and none of us knows exactly how much time we have. Why wait to be happy someday? Why put happiness off until sometime in the future? Why not today? Why not start by adding a bit of happiness every day? Make the decision today, and take a solemn vow that you'll make "someday" really mean right now!

The day I made the decision to buy the sno-cone truck, 'someday' became my 'now.' It took me 54 years, or 19,710 days, to completely say 'yes' to me. When I look at that statement, I can think two ways. I wasted so much time. Or, if my life expectancy is 90, I still have 12,410 days to be happy. My only regret is that I waited so long. But you don't have to.

Don't misunderstand. I am not saying that I have never been happy. I am married to a smart, successful, wonderful, supportive, and loving husband of 27 years. My children bring me great joy and happiness daily: They are my best work on this earth. I have had a fabulous career. I have been to great places, I have wonderful and supportive friends, and I realize how truly blessed I am. I willingly pursued all the education and career opportunities I wanted. I accepted the travel, responsibilities, and paychecks those opportunities offered, and for a long time all of that was great.

[*] https://www.google.com
[**] http://www.absolutely-organized.com/someday-is-not-one-of-the-days-of-the-week

But at some point, it all stopped being fun and great. I missed my husband and my children. I felt worn out and unsatisfied, but I held on for the paycheck and everything it provided until hanging on made me sick. I worried all the time. I am a self-sufficient control freak, so letting go of things was difficult, and letting others help me was really hard. I was carrying so much baggage from the past that I could never live for the joy in the moment. I was trying to keep up with my peers. I believed I was not worthy enough to want anything better. I wasn't optimistic about the future.

To finally wake myself up to take action, it took the deaths of a close friend and my mother and such bad insomnia that the doctor's diagnosis was, "There is nothing I can do for you; you simply must change your lifestyle."

Identifying three things that always made me happy was easy, but having the courage to do something "outside the acceptable box" of my life until then wasn't. Maybe I needed to be a kid again, even for a brief time, because as far back as I can remember, I always felt and acted like an adult. I needed to see what it felt like to be carefree and have fun. The only way to do it was to see all the children's beautiful smiles, hops, skips, and dances, and to listen to the exchanges between preschool pals, discussing, "What do you think is really in a flavor called 'tiger's blood'?"

I needed to see grown men come running out of buildings to a sno-cone truck because it made them feel like kids again. I needed to hear office workers tell me that a sno-cone was the reason they came to work that day! I needed to feel that I was the reason someone smiled—simply because she really wanted a sno-cone but didn't have the money to pay for it, so I gave it away. I needed to comprehend that even in the humblest act, I could make a worthwhile difference to someone, especially after it seemed for so long that all my hard work still had not changed some fundamental things in my life. I had worn myself out trying to be good enough and worthy of love and acceptance. I finally realized I could not look to someone else for love and acceptance, that it had to come from within me.

Dads, love your daughters unconditionally with all your heart. Husbands, if you believed enough in the infinite possibilities of a lifetime together with one woman, believe that she is capable of unlimited possibilities and promise. Mothers, take the superwoman cape off for a minute and let someone help you, take time for yourself, and let your friends nourish and enrich your soul. Don't try to be everything to everyone. Just try to be the best you, and never be ashamed of or apologize for pursuing your passion—whatever it is. Women, support each other.

Set aside time to go away to be alone, and at other times to be only with your spouse, and plan times with your children and friends for pure silliness and fun.

Do something crazy and childlike that you always wanted to do! Describe for yourself what happiness would look like, smell like, sound like, taste like, and feel like!

Take a hop, skip, or a jump into your dream, but for your sake, do something to step toward your goal today. Even that one act, that one step will make you happier.

Understand that once you start moving out of your everyday routine, things may get a little scary; however, believe in yourself and trust that you can do this. Don't be afraid to give of yourself completely—you'll be surprised what comes back to you. Know that everything you experience and learn is making you stronger, smarter, and better. Celebrate each milestone, and give thanks to everyone who helps you along the way. Know that sometimes, even when you feel lost, what you are searching for lies right there within your heart.

Insider tip to success at anything: No matter what your job is, where your dreams take you, what your title may be, what your paystub says, be a Diva at everything you do. You will feel better about yourself, your work will be more enjoyable, you will do better work, others will notice, and they just might do the same thing, so your Diva attitude might become contagious! You might get promoted, and then your job will change, and you'll repeat the process again and again. The simplest way to Diva Status is by doing at least one extraordinary thing each day.

"A diamond is forever." Get clear with yourself and others about who you are, what you want your life to look like, and what core values are just not breakable. Accept that as humans, we are all imperfect and will make mistakes. Discover the value in the lessons you've learned, and keep moving to your brilliant true self. Gain "weight" in the sense of increasing your carats by striving to be a better person, spouse, coworker, and friend. Know and value the few precious people who are gems in your life. Celebrate the memories you create together.

Live your legacy every day of your life. Be genuine and real in your heart about what you want to be remembered for and act accordingly. Remember that the stories others will share most about you will be about how you made them feel.

Define what success means to you, and don't let others' definitions of success define you. Build a solid core within yourself. You will eliminate the need for others' positive opinions or approval. Take away the power that others have over you, and use that power to be you. Be good to yourself, recognize all the good that you have done, and commit to taking care of yourself as well as you take care of others. And let today be the day that you trust, now more than ever, that you are special and good and worthy of peace, joy, and happiness.

ACKNOWLEDGMENTS

THE SWEET ROUTE TO HAPPINESS WAS SCARY, BUMPY, AND NOISY BUT AN adventurous journey with countless moments of happiness along the way. Thank you to all who came along for the ride.

To Juan, Mini Me, my little Boopy, and Chase, the spoiled rotten King Charles Cavalier that lives with us, I love you guys so much. Thank you for letting me be me and for loving, supporting, and encouraging me even when you didn't understand.

To Travis, my new son-in-law, thanks for being a good man, loving Lexi, and agreeing to take care of me in my old age! (Oh, did I just slip that one in?) Remember, it's good to be the king, but it's better to be the queen! Now let me beat you at Scrabble® every now and then.

To Elisa and Nando, for being great friends, awesome people, fun to be with, and generous sponsors of "Operation Sno-Cones & Teddy Bears," the event that ultimately led me to meeting and working with Almon Gunter.

To Almon Gunter, the bold man who climbed into my truck, asked me four questions, and from that conversation, convinced me that I could and should write at least four books, thank you. How exactly did you do that?

To Laura, my partner in crime for all things bold and daring, thank you for supporting me, helping me, and doing things only the best of friends would do. You're the best. To Matt, thank you for all the beautiful art work for this story, and "Stinky" for always bringing me baby love.

To the best wedding planners, Sherri and Trish, who helped me pull off one big, 300-person wedding miracle while I sold sno-cones and wrote a book. Thank you not only for the stupendous day for Lexi and Travis to start their lives together, but for the best day of my life as well. Ladies, you rock!

To Jon and Kathryn Gordon, thanks for reading my manuscript, for giving me a quote to use for this book, and for teaching me to be more grateful for all of life's blessings.

To Jeannette, my financial planner, who guards my money as if it were her own and who works passionately on her mission to help women achieve their best retirement futures, thanks for knowing when to allow me to have my money for an adventure and the courage to say 'no' when an idea isn't fiscally prudent.

And to all my friends who have inspired, coached, motivated, and helped me along this journey, I am truly blessed to have you in my life. I did finally accomplish that goal of writing my first book!! Thank you for holding me accountable to my dream and to my word.

Rolling Double Nickels

It's my birthday, and I am rolling double nickels.
I'm still alive and healthy, and to my heart that tickles!
A half century plus five, so what's all the fuss?
Just one more smart aleck old joke and you'll surely hear me cuss!
At fifty-five, I'm experienced and oh-so-much wiser.
I can get a senior discount and be more of an economizer!
I'm still full of life but would love to retire.
I want to see the world and do things before I expire!
Not quite a bucket yet, my list's more like a shovel and pail.
I want to slow down a bit and take time to exhale.
I want to dig deeper into all life's little treasures.
What I've learned in my lifetime one truly cannot measure!
I am not in middle age anymore; I am in midlife.
Acne, periods, and pregnancy worries are not part of my strife!
I don't have to be a teenager again or fight to keep my boyfriend.
I've learned the importance of apologies and trying to make amends.
So, in essence, life at fifty-five will be just as great!
Remember, fifty-five is still younger than fifty-eight.
Any way you look at it, especially for you men,
Five plus five in any math still equals a perfect ten!
—Abby Vega

Extraordinary Ways to Be Happy in the Moment

Finding money in your jeans, on the street, or in the laundry
Being in the sun
Finding something you want on sale
Getting into bed with fresh sheets
Getting/giving something for free
Performing random acts of kindness
Losing 35 pounds and looking better than you did 30 years ago
Complimenting a stranger
Listening to a favorite song on the radio

Eating chocolate or, in my case, vanilla ice cream
Finding a parking spot up front
Looking at old photos
Avoiding traffic
Receiving praise
Seeing an old friend
Making a list of what makes you happy
Committing to making 'someday' today
Taking a step in the right direction
Letting go
Enjoying the ride

The greatest moments of happiness are those you don't expect to have. Do something unexpected and extraordinary to make someone happy today!

Bibliography

Buckingham, Marcus. November 17, 2009; updated November 17, 2011. "What's Happening to Women's Happiness?" At http://www.huffingtonpost.com/marcus-buckingham/whats-happening-to-womens_b_289511.html.

Buckingham, Marcus. November 23, 2009; updated November 17, 2011. "Women's Happiness: What We Know for Certain." At http://www.huffingtonpost.com/marcus-buckingham/womens-happiness-what-we_b_295876.html.

Crouch, Sacha. 2010. *De-stress Your Success: Get More of What You Want with Less Time, Stress and Effort.* Sydney, AU: Synova Publishing.

Crouch, Sacha. N.d. "How to Let Go of the Need for Approval to Start Thriving." At http://tinybuddha.com/blog/how-to-let-go-of-the-need-for-approval-to-start-thriving.

Fossum, Merle A., and Marilyn J. Mason. [1986] 1989. *Facing Shame: Families in Recovery.* New York: W.W. Norton.

Kaufman, Gershen. 1992. *Shame: The Power of Caring.* Rochester, VT: Schenkman Books, p. 8, quoted by Cooper, Kevin. 2005–2012. *Shame: A Sickness of the Soul.* Santa Rosa, CA: Chinn Street Counseling Center.

Kaufman, Gershen. 1996. *The Psychology of Shame: Theory and Treatment of Shame-Based Syndromes.* (2nd ed.). New York: Springer Publishing.

National Opinion Research Center, University of Chicago. 1972–2014. *The General Social Survey.* At http://www.norc.org/Research/Projects/Pages/general-social-survey.aspx.

Schultz, Danielle. May 25, 2012. "School Counselor Blog: Diva's Day Out!" At http://www.schcounselor.com/2012/05/divas-day-out.html.

Trezise, Katherine, Julie Sarro, and Brigid Fischer. N.d. "'Someday' Is NOT One of the Days of the Week." Absolutely Organized: Professional

Organizing Service. At http://www.absolutely-organized.com/someday-is-not-one-of-the-days-of-the-week.

Ware, Bronnie. November 19, 2009. "The 5 Top Regrets of the Dying." At http://bronnieware.com/regrets-of-the-dying.

Ware, Bronnie. [2011] 2012. *The Top Five Regrets of the Dying: A Life Transformed by the Dearly Departing*. Carlsbad, CA: Hay House.

About the Author

*S*NO-*CONE* *DIARIES: A SWEET ROUTE TO HAPPINESS* IS ABBY VEGA'S FIRST PUB-
lished book. After a 33-year successful and accomplished career in sales,
marketing, senior leadership, personal development, management, training,
and coaching in large corporations, start-ups, and in her own entrepreneurial
endeavors, Abby is thrilled to start yet another chapter in her life as a writer
and motivational speaker.

We know that experiencing positive emotions on a regular basis is vital to our
health and well-being. Because happiness is a personal choice and mindset, this
book outlines a step-by-step process to discover the factors that are holding you
back from achieving happiness. By figuring out what makes you happy, you can
take simple steps daily to turn mundane activities into fun challenges. Abby's true
stories of her adventures at home and on the road with her sno-cone truck teach
us how to turn the unexpected pleasures in life that make us smile every day into
tools to help us build happier, more meaningful lives for ourselves and others.

Abby has lived in Ponte Vedra Beach, Florida, for 20 years with her husband
of 27 years Juan, daughter Alexis (and now, son-in-law Travis), son Justin, dad
Robert, and their King Charles Cavalier Spaniel, Chase.

CPSIA information can be obtained
at www.ICGtesting.com
Printed in the USA
FSOW03n0140030117
29140FS

9 780981 479590